Anonymous

Report Presented at the Annual Meeting of the Thirteenth Anniversary

Of the New South Wales Institution for the Deaf and Dumb and the Blind...

Anonymous

Report Presented at the Annual Meeting of the Thirteenth Anniversary
Of the New South Wales Institution for the Deaf and Dumb and the Blind...

ISBN/EAN: 9783744763257

Printed in Europe, USA, Canada, Australia, Japan

Cover: Foto ©ninafisch / pixelio.de

More available books at **www.hansebooks.com**

REPORT

Annual Meeting of the Thirteenth Anniversary

OF THE

New South Wales Institution

FOR THE

DEAF and DUMB, and the BLIND,

For the Year Ending 30th September, 1874,

WITH

THE TREASURER'S BALANCE SHEETS,

LISTS OF DONATIONS AND SUBSCRIPTIONS,

AND

The Rules and Regulations of the Institution.

JOSEPH COOK & CO., PRINTERS, 370, GEORGE STREET,
OPPOSITE THE BANK OF NEW SOUTH WALES.

1874.

OFFICE BEARERS AND COMMITTEE

For the year ending 30th September, 1875.

Patron :
HIS EXCELLENCY SIR HERCULES ROBINSON, K.C.B., &c.

President :
THE REV. GEORGE KING, M.A.

Vice-President :
THE REV. DR. LANG.

Hon. Treasurer :
HENRY PHILLIPS, ESQ.

Hon. Secretary :
ELLIS ROBINSON, ESQ.
486, George-street, Sydney.

Hon. Surgeon :
ARTHUR RENWICK, ESQ., M.D.

Committee :

E. T. BEILBY, ESQ.	ALDERMAN LINSLEY, J.P.
S. C. BROWN, ESQ., M.L.A.	W. LOVE, ESQ., J.P.
JOHN FRAZER, ESQ.	REV. JAMES MILNE, M.A.
J. R. FAIRFAX, ESQ.	WILLIAM RAE, ESQ.
ROBERT HILLS, ESQ.	F. R. ROBINSON, ESQ.
JAMES HENRY, ESQ.	GEORGE F. WISE, ESQ.

Ladies' Visiting Committee :

MRS. BAILLIE,	MRS. STANGER LEATHES,
MRS. BARRY,	MRS. M. METCALFE,
MRS. BREILLAT,	MISS MACKIE,
MRS. BALCOMBE,	LADY MANNING,
MRS. DUNSMURE,	MRS. NOTT,
MRS. J. H. GOODLET,	MRS. F. R. ROBINSON,
MRS. JOHN HAY,	MRS. W. SCOTT,
MRS. ROBERT HILLS,	MRS. GEORGE F. WISE.
MRS. GEORGE KING,	

Master :
MR. SAMUEL WATSON.

Matron :	**Matron's Assistant :**
MRS. ASHTON.	MISS CAMPBELL.
Music Teacher :	**Clerk & Collector :**
MISS C. SHARP, L.A.M.,	MR. GEORGE LUFF.

Pupil Teacher :
CHRISTINA CAMERON.

The Institution is open to Subscribers and other Visitors daily, from 2 until 4 o'clock, p.m., Saturdays, Sundays, and Holidays excepted.

Life Directors.

APPOINTED UNDER RULE IV.

Clause 1.

KING, REV. GEORGE, M.A. | ROBINSON, F. R. ESQ.
LOVE, WILLIAM, ESQ., J.P.

Clause 2.

ROBINSON, ELLIS, ESQ.

Clause 3.

LANG, REV. DR. | FRAZER, JOHN, ESQ., J. P.

Clause 4.

BELMORE, His Excellency The Right Hon. Earl of
PAXTON, JOSEPH, ESQ. | WOOD, JOHN W., ESQ.
WALKER, THOMAS, ESQ. | HOLTERMANN, B. O., ESQ.

Clause 5.

JOY, EDWARD, ESQ. | WISE, GEORGE F., ESQ.

Names of Donors of £50 and upwards in aid of the Funds of the Institution.

His Excellency the Right Hon. Earl of Belmore, Donations £350.

Fairfax and Sons...	Donation	£100	Thomas Walker ...	Donation	£200
Mrs. Mary Roberts	,,	100	William Manson...	Bequest	100
James Williams ...	Bequest	100	William Keel ...	,,	150
Maurice Alexander	,,	50	John W. Wood ...	Donation	100
Dr. Charles Muller	...Don.	100	B. O. Holterman ...	,,	100
Hon. John Frazer	... ,,	50	Joseph Paxton, J.P.	,,	50
Bryan Fawl	Bequest	50	Hamilton Hume ...	Bequest	50

William Moffitt, Bequest £250.

RESOLUTIONS

Passed at the Thirteenth Annual Meeting held at the New Institution
Newtown Road, on Monday Afternoon, 12th October, 1874.

The Hon. John Hay, M.L.C., in the Chair.

Moved by Rev. G. King,
Seconded by Mr. Paxton :—

"That the Report now read be adopted, and, together with the Balance
Sheets be printed for circulation."—Carried unanimously.

Moved by Rev. Dr. Steel,
Seconded by Mr. G. F. Wise :—

"That the thanks of this Meeting are hereby given to the Government and
Parliament for the annual donation of £450, in aid of the Funds of the
Institution."—Carried unanimously.

Moved by Rev. Daniel Allen,
Seconded by Rev. J. Galloway :—

"That the following gentlemen do constitute the Committee for the ensuing
year :—*President*, the Rev. George King, M.A.; *Vice-President*, Rev. Dr.
Lang; *Hon. Treasurer*, Mr. Henry Phillips; *Hon. Secretary*, Mr. Ellis
Robinson; *Hon. Surgeon*, Mr. Arthur Renwick, M.D.; *Committee*, Mr. E.
T. Beilby, Mr. S. C. Brown, M.L.A., Mr. John Frazer, Mr. J. R. Fairfax,
Mr. Robert Hills, Mr. James Henry, Alderman Linsley, J.P., Mr. W. Love, J.P.,
Rev. James Milne, M.A., Mr. William Rae, Mr. F. R. Robinson, Mr. George
F. Wise."

THIRTEENTH ANNUAL REPORT

OF THE

NEW SOUTH WALES

Institution for the Deaf & Dumb & the Blind,

For the Year ending September 30th, 1874.

TO THE SUBSCRIBERS.

Another year has passed, and it becomes the duty of the Committee to report to the Subscribers the progress and position of the Institution.

THE PROGRESS OF THE PUPILS.

This they are happy to state continues very satisfactory, and many of the elder scholars are attaining a high degree of efficiency. At the Annual Examination held last December, the expressions of approval elicited from the large audience were most encouraging, and the distribution of prizes then made has been the means of causing the amount of emulation among the pupils. The Music teaching has been satisfactory, but the few Blind Scholars in the Institution who have any ear at all for Music, does not give much choice of pupils; one of the most forward also has left during the past year.

HEALTH OF THE PUPILS.

Four months since Scarlet Fever of a mild type broke out; six cases occurred; but the means at command, and the large accommodation of the Institution affording facilities for the isolation of the patients, together with the liberal use of disinfectants, and the assiduous attention of our Hon. Surgeon, Dr. Renwick, the skilful nursing of the Matron and assistant, contributed to their speedy recovery, and prevented the infection spreading through the Institution; the Committee gladly take this opportunity of thanking Dr. Renwick. The children are all now in excellent health.

Number of Inmates.

The number of children in the Institution at the end of last year was 59, and there has been received since, two boys and one girl. Two of these from Tasmania, and one from New South Wales, making a total of 62 ; of this number nine have left for their homes and friends—six deaf and dumb, and three blind— and there now remains in the Institution 53,—43 deaf and dumb, and 10 blind, some applications for admission are now pending. One of the blind boys who left, was apprenticed by the Committee to a chair caner, and a sample of his and other work from the Institution, was awarded a Bronze Medal at the last Intercolonial Exhibition.

Financial.

Though the Subscriptions have not increased proportionally to the expenditure; the Institution, however, is becoming more known, and occupies a firmer and more satisfactory position among the charitable public. Of the special receipts the Committee would beg to notice the following :—

Bequest of William Moffitt, Esq.	..£250	0	0
„ Maurice Alexander, Esq. ...	50	0	0
„ Hamilton Hume, Esq.	50	0	0
„ George Copas, Esq....	25	0	0
From W. B. Campbell, Esq., Portion of proceeds of Exhibition Fancy Fair...	54	15	7
„ Mr. O'Neil, Queanbeyan, Collected by	40	1	0

The payments for School Fees and Clothing are satisfactory, being £333 10s. 3d. for this year, against £372 3s. 4d. for last year.

The Country collections have also been highly gratifying, and during the travels of the Country Collector, several new pupils have been forwarded to the Institution.

Improvements and Additions.

The sanguine hopes expressed in last year's report have been fulfilled, and the balance to credit of Building Fund was so much increased in the early part of this year as to enable the Committee to carry out the urgently required additions and improvements then mentioned, viz., the erection of the Balconies and

Verandahs around the Building—these seven in number, two Balconies and five Verandahs, with new Fuel house, &c., &c., are now completed, the work having been carried out under the supervision of the Architect of the Building, in a most substantial manner, the whole of the timber used being hardwood. The cost of the whole of the addition has been a trifle over £1,000, one thousand pounds, and your inspection is invited.

These last additions have proved a very great boon during the late boisterous winter weather, and will largely tend to protect the main building.

The whole of the border of the grounds against the fences has been trenched, and is now planted with trees and shrubs, a donation from the Botanical Gardens.

LADY VISITORS.

The Ladies' Visiting Committee, consisting of the under mentioned ladies; namely, Mrs. Baillie, Mrs. Breillat, Mrs. Barry, Mrs. Balcombe, Mrs. Dunsmure, Mrs. Goodlet, Mrs. John Hay, Mrs. Hills, Mrs. George King, Mrs. Leathes, Mrs. Metcalfe, Miss Mackie, Lady Manning, Mrs. Nott, Mrs. F. R. Robinson, Mrs. Scott, Mrs. Wise, who continue their good offices with much benefit to the Institution.

VISIT OF ROYAL COMMISSIONERS.

The gentlemen appointed as a Royal Commission to report upon the charities of the colony, paid a visit of Inspection in due course to this Institution, and in their most exhaustive and able report notified their impressions as being most satisfactory, and the following extract from the Second Report of the Commissioners appointed to inquire into, and report upon, the Working and Management of the Public Charities of the Colony, 29th May, 1874, page 117 :—

" The Institution for the Deaf and Dumb and the Blind.—This Institution being to a small extent assisted by a Parliamentary vote, we made an inquiry into its management. We found it contained Twenty-one Deaf and Dumb Boys, and an equal number of Girls of the same class, besides Five Blind Boys and Seven Blind girls. The management appeared to us to be good, and we remarked nothing calling for particular notice. The Institution is conducted on unsectarian principles, and from its truly charitable character, is in every way deserving of public support."

General Remarks.

Among the many kind services and Donations during the year the following deserve especial notification, namely :—Free admission to the Great Hibernicon at the School of Arts. Mr. J. F. Staff, Parramatta Picnic to Chowder Bay, to celebrate his golden wedding. Mr. Elonis, Inspection of the Mint and machinery in motion. St. Stephen's Picnic, per Rev. Robert Taylor. Picnic to Rose Bay, kindly given by Mrs. John Hay, and a large Christmas tree handsomely decorated by Mrs. Wise and other ladies,—with numerous presents and toys provided for each of the children by Mr. Elonis.

The numerous other Donations of Fruit, Vegetables, &c., will be given in full in the report.

The Committee have to record with deep regret the death of one of their valued members, the late Maurice Alexander, Esq., whose kind attention to the wants of the Inmates, and to the interests of the Institution generally, had endeared him to all its members.

Conclusion.

In concluding their report the Committee again commend the Institution and its Inmates to the care of Almighty God, to whom they desire to offer their heartfelt thanks for the continued success which He has permitted to attend their efforts on behalf of the afflicted objects of their care.

The Institution is open daily, except Saturday and Sunday, from 2 to 4 o'clock for visitors, who are invited to inspect and see for themselves, the manner in which it is carried on; the method of Instruction will be explained by some of the Teachers.

Institution for the Deaf and Dumb, and the Blind,
Newtown Road.

COMPOSITION BY THE PUPILS.

The following specimens of composition, or essays are the work of some of the elder pupils, (the subjects are of their own choosing) and receive no correction except such as their respective writers can make on a careful review, when the prominent errors are pointed out by a Teacher. In judging then it is well to remember the ages of the writers, and the length of time at school. And that very few if any had acquired a knowledge of written or spoken language previously to their admission to the Institution.

By J. S.
ABOUT FRANCE.

France is bounded on the North by the British Channel ; South by Spain and the Gulf of Lyons ; West by the Bay of Biscay ; East by Prussia. Paris is the Capital of France. Paris is a very beautiful city. The Prussians fought against the French lately. Napoleon I. lived in France. He died at St. Helena, A.D. 1821. The chief rivers of France are, Rhone, Seine, &c. The chief towns of it are, Paris, Bordeaux, Bouen, Nantes, Havre. It is a very fertile country. There are many grapes in it. The grapes are made into Wine. Napoleon III. fled from France to England. There are many Roman Catholics and few Protestants in it. Lyons is noted for silk manufactures.

By A. P.
THE TYPES OF JESUS CHRIST.

Jesus Christ is the Great Antitype. A type is a likeness of some person or thing to come called the Antitype. Joshua, Moses, Jonah, Joseph, David, Adam, and Isaac, &c., were types of Jesus Christ. Joshua was a leader of the Israelites from the Wilderness into Canaan ; so Jesus Christ leads believers to heaven. Moses led the Israelites from the bondage of Egypt through the wilderness ; so Jesus Christ leads believers from the slavery of sin and satan to the liberty of God's children. Jonah was three days and three nights in the whale's belly ; so Jesus Christ was three days and three nights in the grave. Joseph was hated and sold by his brethren ; so Christ was hated by His brethren and sold by Judas. David says, "I was as a deaf man that heard not, and I was as a dumb man that openeth not his mouth," because the wicked people were cruel and rude to him ; so Jesus Christ was dumb and He did not open His mouth before Pontius Pilate. Noah's Ark, Jacob's Ladder, the Brazen Serpent were things typical of Christ. Noah's family were saved in the Ark ; so Jesus Christ will save believers from God's wrath. Jacob's Ladder prefigured Jesus Christ who is the only Way to the Father, and the one Mediator between God and men. The people who looked to the Brazen Serpent were healed ; so believers who look in faith to Jesus Christ shall be saved. Types were useful to teach the Jews to look to Christ, "The Lamb of God who should come to take away the sin of the world."

By J. G.
ABOUT INDIA.

India is bounded on the North by the Himaleh Mountains ; South by Palk's Strait ; East by the Bay of Bengal ; West by the Arabian Sea. It is about 1,900 miles long, and 1,600 miles broad. Its area is 1,200,000 square miles.

The chief towns of India are, Calcutta, Madras, Bombay. The three Presidencies of India are, Bengal, Madras, and Bombay. Calcutta is situated on the river Hoogly. The chief rivers of India are Ganges, Godavery, Indus, &c. They flow into the Bay of Bengal. The productions of India are, Indigo, cotton, sugar, opium, cocoanut, &c. Cape Comorin is south of India. The chief gulfs are called, Gulfs of Combay and Cutch. The religion of India is chiefly Buddhism. It belongs to England. About 146 Englishmen were shut in a small room called the Blackhole, in the reign of George II. Next morning 123 were found dead. Lord Mayo the late Governor, was killed by the natives. Mr. Joy visited India lately. Women cast their babies into the river Ganges. They are ignorant and cruel. We pity them. India is called the old world. The climate of India is hot near the Equator. India is a very rich and fertile country. There are many wild animals in India. The Hindoos are slight and graceful. The poor people wear scanty clothing, but the women wear rings of gold or silver. The manufactures of Hindostan are numerous. The Indian shawls are remarkable for their beauty. The population of India is 180 millions. Some Missionaries are teaching the heathen there. Some heathens are converted to Christianity. We pray God to convert the heathen.

By A. McD.
ABOUT SPAIN.

Spain is bounded North by the Bay of Biscay; South by the Mediterranean Sea and Strait of Gibraltar; West by Atlantic Ocean and Portugal; East by the Mediterranean Sea. Madrid is the capital of Spain. The chief towns of Spain are, Madrid, Saragossa, Cadiz, Bracelona, &c. The chief rivers of Spain are, Douro, Tagus, &c. The chief mountains of Spain are, Castilians and Toledo mountains, &c. There are many monkeys in Spain. The Strait of Gibraltar is between Spain and Africa. There are some Protestants and many Roman Catholics in Spain. The English fought against the Spaniards. The English prayed God to help them. So God sent a storm and destroyed the ships. The population of Spain is about 15 millions. Spain is about 640 miles long, and 530 miles broad. The climate of it is temperate. It is divided into 49 Provinces. The Spaniards are very dark in the complexion. The Spanish language is difficult. The Government of Spain is now in a disturbed state. Amdeus was the king of Spain. Spaniards are fond of music and dancing. There are now cruel fights in Spain. The Spaniards were very active formerly. There are many figs, mulberries, &c. The sky and climate of Spain are beautiful.

By E. H.
ABOUT HENRY II.

Henry II. was born at Mons in Normandy. He began to reign A.D. 1154. He reigned 34¾ years. He was the son of Geoffrey. He married Eleanor. She was a haughty, jealous, and worthless woman. He was crowned three times, at Worcester, Westminster, and at Lincoln. He was a man of low stature, of much learning and courage, but proud and revengeful. He had five sons, named William, Henry, Richard, John, and Geoffrey. He invaded Ireland A.D. 1171. Pope Adrian IV. had granted Ireland to Henry A.D. 1172. The Pope soon quarrelled with him. The Pope loved Thomas A'Becket. He was Archbishop of Canterbury. He was at first Chancellor of England. Four knights murdered him at the altar of St. Benedict, Canterbury. He took William I. of Scotland and put him in prison. Fair Rosamond was poisoned by Queen Eleanor. He belonged to the Plantagenets. Pope Adrian IV. was chocked by a fly A.D. 1159. Glass was first used for windows A.D. 1180. He created his son John Lord of Ireland. Ireland was divided into five kingdoms then named, Leinster, Meath, Ulster, Munster, and Connaught. He died of his broken heart because of the ingratitude of his sons, and was buried at Font Evard in Anjou.

By M. J. C.
ABOUT HENRY I.

Henry I. was born at Selby in Yorkshire. He began to reign A.D. 1100. He reigned 35 years. He was the youngest son of William the Conqueror. He married Matilda, daughter of Malcolm of Scotland, and niece of Edgar Atheling. He united the Saxon and Norman Lines. He had William who was drowned coming from Normandy A.D. 1120, and Matilda who was married to Henry V., of Germany A.D. 1109. He was brave and learned, but cruel and unjust. He put a stop to the Curfew Bell A.D. 1100. He changed many of the laws which were offensive to the people. He invaded Normandy and defeated his brother Robert, and took him a prisoner A.D. 1107. His eyes were put out and he was kept as a prisoner in Cardiff Castle for 28 years. The Knights Templars were established A.D. 1118. The manufactures of woollen cloth began in this reign by a company of Flemish weavers. Henry I. died after having eaten too many lampreys. He was buried at Reading Abbey A.D. 1135.

By F. H.
ABOUT MOSES.

Moses was born in Egypt. He was the Son of Jochebed and Amram. He was hid in the ark of bulrushes on the River Nile by his parents for three months. Pharaoh's daughter found him in the cradle on the Nile and she brought him to the King of Egypt. He killed an Egyptian and he fled to Midian. God appeared to him in the burning bush. The bush was not consumed. God told him to go to King Pharaoh. He asked Pharaoh to let the Jews go from Egypt but he refused. Moses cast a rod on the ground and it became a serpent. God sent the ten plagues on Egypt. He led the Jews through the Red Sea on the dry ground. The Egyptians were drowned in the Red Sea. He married Zipporah who was daughter of Jethro. Jethro was the High Priest of Midian. Jethro was the father in law of Moses. He was a Shepherd of Midian. He had two sons who were named Gershon and Eleazar. He went up to Mount Sinai. God gave him the ten commandments. He prayed God to send quails and manna to the Jews. The Jews murmured against Moses. He smote the rock twice, and the water came out and followed the Jews. They drank of it. The Rock was a type of Christ. Korah, Dathan and their sons rebelled against Moses and Aaron. The sons Korah and Dathan were swallowed up in the Earth. He died on Mount Nebo. God buried him in a valley in the land of Moab. The Jews were sorry when Moses died. Joshua, the son of Nun, was appointed to lead the Jews into Canaan.

By W. E.
ABOUT GEORGE I.

George I. was born in Hanover. He began to reign A.D. 1714. He reigned 12 years in England. He married his cousin Sophia Dorotha daughter of George of Denmark. He had two children George who succeeded him and Sophia who married the King of Prussia. He imprisoned his wife during 40 years in Hanover. He fought against Spain A.D. 1718. James Edward Stuart Son of James II. called the Old Pretenders raised a rebellion against George I, A.D. 1715. He landed in England at Peterhead 22nd December A.D. 1715. The Spanish fleet was defeated at Cape Passaro in Sicely by General Byng A.D. 1718. James died at Rome, A.D. 1765. The Irish people greatly disliked George I. Dr. Isaac Watts died A.D. 1749. George I died of apoplexy in his carriage near Onsbruck while on a journey to Hanover. He was buried at Hanover. The English were not very sorry when he died.

By A. W.

ABOUT PAUL.

Saul was born at Tarsus. He was cruel at first. He killed the Christians by order of the High Priest. He went to seek and put the Christians in prison. Some of them were put to death. He was converted on his way to Damascus. He fell to the ground. He heard a voice saying " Saul, Saul why persecutest thou me." He said " Who art thou Lord." The Lord said " I am Jesus." Saul's name was changed into Paul. He said " What wilt thou have me to do. The Lord said he must arise and preach about Christ at Jerusalem at first. Christ was kind and talked with him. He was three days without sight or food. The Lord told Ananias to go and talk to Paul. Ananias put his hands on Paul. He received his sight. He was weak and hungry because he had not eaten or drank for three days. He received meat to eat and he was strengthened. He became a good apostle of Christ. He believed in Christ and preached Christ in the Synagogue. The Jews heard him preaching. They watched the gates day and night to kill him. The disciples took him by night and let him down by the wall in a basket. He was with the good disciples. He met and accompanied the disciple Barnabas. He preached the gospels to the Gentiles. He warned the Jews because they crucified Christ who was without sin. He wrote 14 epistles. He was put in prison with Silas. Paul said to the Gaoler " Believe on the Lord Jesus Christ and thou shalt be saved and thy house." He raised Eutychus from the dead. He went through different countries. Felix trembled at Paul's preaching. The people of Athens were ignorant. Paul was sorry because they worshipped an idol, " To the Unknown god." Paul taught them to worship the true God. The people at Malta told him God was angry with him because the viper was on his hand. Paul put off the viper and did not feel hurt. They then said he was like a God. He did not seek the praise of men. He loved Christ. They loved Paul. They cried much because Paul was gone. He cried also. He went to Rome. He preached Christ when he was in the court. He did not fear the King. He had many sufferings on the earth. He has joys in heaven. He did not fear to die. He met Christ in heaven. He was beheaded by the order of Nero. Nero was a wicked king.

By C. C.

THE RESURRECTION.

Resurrection means bringing to life again that which was dead. In it the dead shall be raised. They will rise at the end of the world. Christ raised the dead to life by His own power and in His own name. Elijah, Elishua, Paul and the apostles raised the dead to life. They did not work miracles by their own power or name but Christ's power and help. Elijah raised the son of a widow at Sarepta.

Elisha raised the son of the Shummanite to life. Paul raised Eutychus to life. Eutychus was a young man who fell asleep when Paul was preaching so long. He fell off the third loft. Paul embraced him and he lived again. Peter restored Dorcas to life. Peter said "Rise Tabitha. Our Saviour restored Lazarus, Jarius's daughter and a widows son of Nain to life. "The dead shall hear the voice of the Archangel and the trump of God."

They shall be raised by Christ at the last day. Our bodies shall be corruption. The righteous will have glorious bodies at the Resurrection. As the seed is planted and corrupts; so shall our bodies become corrupt. And as beautiful new plants grow up. So the righteous shall have glorious bodies. As Christ rose from the dead so we shall be raised likewise. The Sadduccees said that there would no resurrection, neither spirits nor angels. They said "persons would perish as the beasts and would never be raised again. Our Saviour reproved them for unbelief. We read the beautiful texts about the resurrection in fifteenth chapter of 1 Corinthians. St. Paul wrote it.

SPEECHES AND PROCEEDINGS

AT THE

THIRTEENTH ANNUAL PUBLIC MEETING.

Extracted from the daily Press.

———o———

The annual meeting in connection with this Institution took place yesterday afternoon, in the large hall of the edifice on the Newtown Road. The building was quite filled with the children, their teachers, and the visitors—about nine-tenths of the latter being ladies. The chair was taken by the Hon. John Hay, President of the Legislative Council, and amongst others upon the platform were the Rev. George King, M.A. (President), Revs. Dr. Steel, J. Galloway, C. Stewart, D. Allen, S. F. M'Kenzie, Messrs. F. R. Robinson, J. Paxton, J. Henry, G. F. Wise, W. Love, and Ellis Robinson. The ladies included amongst them Lady Robinson (accompanied by Mrs. Dick), Mrs. Goodlet, Mrs. Hay, Mrs. Scott, Miss Holt, Miss Mackie, the Misses King, &c. Apologies were received from Sir Alfred Stephen, Mrs. Goodenough, and Mrs. Metcalfe.

The CHAIRMAN, in opening the proceedings, said that it had been customary for many years back to have the advantage of the Governor's presence at these meetings; and he was sure they all regretted very much that his Excellency, being engaged upon important public business elsewhere, could not show that interest in the institution on the present occasion which he had hitherto done. He (Mr. Hay) presumed that he had been asked to take the chair more in consequence of the position he had the honour to hold in connection with Parliament than for any particular merit or claim in connection with this institution, although he had always taken a warm interest in it from the beginning. Still he knew that there were many other gentlemen in the town who had much greater claim than he had to the honour accorded him on this occasion. It afforded him great pleasure to show the interest he took in this institution; indeed he felt that there could not possibly be an institution of an eleemosynary nature which more deserved the thanks of all classes of the community. It was one of those things which made us thankful that we live in this age of the world to observe how much the spirit of humanity had increased since the earlier epochs. The greatest philosopher and the greatest observer of ancient times had pronounced absolutely that the deaf and dumb were precluded from improvement, and could not be taught the exercise of the reasoning powers of man; and in all other writers of antiquity there was very little mention of the deaf and dumb, besides the most cruel dictum. These unfortunates had apparently been totally neglected and treated with contempt, except in those instances where they were the subject of superstitious fear as being under evil influences. The children of the rich were shut away from public observation as much as possible, while the children of the poor were made little better than the beasts of burden. It was something in this age to see the different way in which these poor creatures were viewed, how much they possessed of the reasoning powers, how much of the intellect as well as the heart of man they were capable of developing, and to see that science and the efforts of philanthropic individuals had overcome all the difficulties which stood in the way of imparting the instruction desired. It was not until the fifteenth century of the Christian era that any notion got abroad that it was possible to teach the deaf and dumb, and they were left altogether unprovided for. But about that period, in the awakening of the intellect of Europe, the spirit of humanity and of Christianity being active, the minds of many of the philanthropic began to be exercised as to whether something could not be done to relieve those afflicted with these infirmities; and from that time various methods had been adopted, which had eventually resulted in an almost effectual system for imparting education to the deaf and dumb. We now stirring in this new country felt the advantages of the system established at home. Fourteen years ago this institution had made a commencement in a very humble way; and he recollected that as far back as 1865 the children domiciled in it only amounted to ten. There were now fifty-two deaf and dumb, besides ten blind children, within its walls, and it was thus manifest that very great progress indeed had been made. He was very glad to see that by one of the rules the founders were placed at the head of the list of members as life-directors. He was glad to see three of them present, the Rev. George King and Messrs. Love and Robinson; these gentlemen must have reason to be proud of the result of the humble beginning made some twelve or fourteen years ago. They had great reason to be grateful also to one now no longer amongst us, the Earl of Belmore. As Lord Belmore had left the colony, and was not likely to return again the time had come to admit the great debt of gratitude the institution was under to that nobleman. (Cheers.) It had been proposed to call this institution by Lord Belmore's name; but it was, perhaps wisely, decided not to do so. He was quite sure, however, that they ought to be very much ashamed of themselves if they did not acknowledge the great advantages the institution had derived from the Earl's liberality and patronage, extended, indeed, not only to this but to all the charitable institutions of the country. At the time when his rev. friend Mr. King had despaired of being able to obtain sufficient money to raise a permanent institution, Lord Belmore generously headed a subscription which in about eighteen months enabled this building to be completed—almost to the astonishment and surprise of those most intimately connected with it and most anxious to see it prosper. Another great advantage had been secured by obtaining the services of so excellent and able a teacher as they had in Mr. Watson. (Hear, hear.) It was impossible to overrate the advantages of having so devoted a teacher, so able in what might be called his profession, and so excellent a man, in every way deserving of encouragement and approbation. He was glad to observe by the report that this establishment still flourished, that its inmates were in admirable health, making good progress, and that the funds were such as to enable the purposes to be carried out to as great an extent as was at the present time desired. No effort should be spared on the part of those who took an interest in the institution to get the greatest support which could be secured from the public. This was one of those institutions which (as Sir Hercules Robinson had remarked at the last annual meeting) you could not possibly over-do. There were many charitable institutions which, however laudable their desire, you might have some hesitation in according your support to; you might possibly consider that you were doing more harm than good by encouraging tbat which it was desired to overcome or repress. But in this case you could not by any possibility do harm; you could not increase tbe number of those who might perhaps be your future care. Emissaries should be sent out in all directions, not merely to collect subscriptions, but to get in all who might be the objects of tbe charity. Their mission would not be completed until every deaf and dumb cbild in tbe colony was under their influence. Yet however much they might do for them, they would not add one unfortunate to tho list of those whom they sought to redeem. He wished to encourage those who had taken so great an interest in the cause; they knew as well as he did that much had been done, but very much still remained. They ought to have the guardianship over tbe objects of their solicitude not only in their youth but in after life; they should be apprenticed out to different trades, which might enable them to make tbeir living, and have all that happiness which could only arise from earning one's own livelihood. This was for the future; from what bad been done in the past there could not be any doubt that this institution would continue to be a success, and that it would go on until it fairly competed with what had been done in the same way either in the sister colonies or in Great Britain. As Sir Hercules Robinson had said at the last meeting, this institution had a peculiar charm upon the community, because it was unsectarian. It was one of those things in which all clergymen, of whatever denomination, should unite to bring children. But although it was unsectarian, he was sure that it was an institution imbued with the spirit of religion, and he hoped it would always remain so, for it would be sad indeed if we were practically to open the eyes and ears of these unfortunate children submitted to our care, and nothing were to be imparted to them upon which they might lean for consolation iu this life, and look for happiness in the future. (Cheers.) He called upon the hon. secretary to read the annual report.

Mr. ELLIS ROBINSON, honorary secretary read the following report and balance-sheet:—Which appears in previous pages.

Rev. G. KING said that in passing among the inmates of this institution he was asked by a gentleman the following question:—"Which of the two afflictions, that of the blind or of the deaf and dumb, did he consider the heavier affliction?" It was difficult for those who have never realised in themselves either of those privations to arrive at a just appreciation of the state of those two afflicted classes. On the one hand, the deaf and dumb are shut out from all social communion. The two grand avenues which mankind possess for the reception and communication of ideas are absolutely closed against them. Darkness rests upon the mind; a worse than Egyptian darkness envelops the soul. No human voice has ever reached that ear, no sweet music has ever awakened within that dull, cold breast the melody of song. All the faculties of the soul are dormant, and life is one long, dreary, melancholy blank. To the blind, on the other hand, all external nature is blotted out of existence. In vain for them the glorious sun arises, and fills all nature with light and life and joy. The trees may stand forth to us in all their varied beauty of light and shade, the bright leaves sparkling in the sunshine, the graceful branches waving in the breeze, the sweet bloom of bud and flower, the rich ripening fruit, the gladsome birds upon the wing, the cattle upon a thousand hills, the flocks and herds browsing upon the undulating plain, the rich green carpet jewelled with flowers of exquisite beauty, the lofty mountain-peak towering in the skies, and the mighty ocean sublime in its calm and peaceful smiles, as well as in the upheaving of its mountain waves. All this melody of earth and sea and sky, which thrills the soul with gladness, and speaks to us of our one great Father who first said "Let them be," and they were, and who still preserves them in all their freshness by His gracious providence—all these liveried servants of our beneficent Creator may minister unceasingly to our enjoyments, but to the blind they are silent and unseen. All their glory is sepulchred in darkness, and death reigns around. Such, to the blind, the loss of this one sense! Now, to the deaf and dumb all those rich stores of nature are open before their eyes, but to their benighted mind, her wealth of beauty and knowledge is written in cipher; they have no key to open up her treasures. They see, but perceive not. The fact is, the beauty and knowledge which come to us from nature is not inherent there. Its source is in the soul of man. The fountain of inspiration is within. The light emanates originally from the human soul upon the outspread field of nature, and by reflection flows back again in ten thousand beauteous channels, joyous with all nature's freshness, and hallowed in the recognition of our heavenly Father's goodness in the midst of it all. While we thus enjoy the glory of our Father's rich domain, these afflicted children can but stand at that closed-up sepulchre, and, with the weeping Mary, drop a tear in sad and melancholy loneliness. O! would that with the angel we could come and roll away the stone, and offer to our afflicted brethren a word of consolation. 'Tis to this angelic work that your attention was invited here this afternoon. That bright spirit with the light of heaven upon her wings is but an emblem of the mission which in the strength of Providence this institution had undertaken. The first object which presented itself to their attention on stepping over the threshold of this building was the inscription over the doorway in these words : " Then the eyes of the blind shall be opened, and the ears of the deaf shall be unstopped." This beautiful allegorical prophecy, after a lapse of a millennium and a half, we recognised in these happy children developed into a realised fact. Through the teaching of this institution God had given utterance to that beneficent command, " Ephatha "—be opened, and the eye, long sealed in darkness, opened to the mental, moral, and spiritual world. The deaf ear is unstopped ; the tongue of the dumb was released from bondage, and all the glorious things of heaven and earth, once sepulchred in death, were now revealed to the intellect and brought home to the soul of those happy inmates. In this labour of love the institution had so far worked with the success which they were now able to witness and attest. Both afflictions, no doubt, are grievous beyond our powers of expression ; but both classes after a few years of instruction here, are returned to their homes intellectual and industrious, cheerful and happy ; or, if friendless and homeless, they still have a happy home in the institution until provision is made for their earning a comfortable and independent living by the use of their own hands or heads. Here now was an opportunity for our bearing a part in this hallowed mission ; and it should be a part worthy of the cause, and worthy of ourselves. He was happy to be able to state, also, that they had in some measure realised the hope which he gave expression to at the last annual meeting with reference to the adult blind and deaf and dumb of Sydney. They had been all visited in their own houses by Mr. Watson, the master of the institution, and some of them are now under his instruction. He had also visited some of the deaf and dumb adults, and communicated our views with regard to them. What we want to do for the adults is this : To teach them some industrial trade, and to supply them with materials for carrying on industrial pursuits in their own homes. For this department of the society's work additional means must be raised. · But past experience had assured them that they might trust to the generosity of the charitable public. It was only necessary to mention the wants of a good cause, like the present, in order to have those wants abundantly supplied. Mr. Watson had already communicated instruction to these adult blind and deaf and dumb ; every Sunday morning he met and instructed them, in which labour he was supported by some good young men, one a blind young man partially educated here, and two young men belonging to the Christian Association. He was sure that they might confidently rely upon the support necessary to carry on this good work. In conclusion, he had much pleasure in moving,—"That the report now read be adopted, and, together with the treasurer's balance-sheet, be printed and circulated."

Mr. JOSEPH PAXTON, J.P., seconded.

The motion was put and carried unanimously.

Rev. Dr. STEEL moved the second Resolution,—"That the thanks of this meeting be given to the Government and Parliament for the annual grant of £450 in aid of the funds of this institution." It was very desirable that while so many were willing to give help voluntarily, the Government and Parliament should secure from the taxes of the country what might be termed involuntary help. It concerned the whole country very much that this should be done ; in fact it might be called a matter of education. The deaf and dumb and the blind were endowed with the same faculties as we were, but they laboured under an immense disadvantage in developing them, and it was to overcome that that the struggle was made. Coming from European stock we might be supposed to have much the same proportion of deaf mutes amongst us namely, one in every 1600. In the United Kingdom the average was about one in every 1650 ; in the mountainous districts of Scotland, one in 1300. These freaks of nature, so to speak, appearing very striking as we instituted a comparison of the numbers in which they were developed in different localities. In Yorkshire the average was one in every 2331 ; in Worcestershire one in 1160 ; whereas in Switzerland, as any traveller could not fail to observe, there was no less than one in every 200. We might be supposed to have taken the European rate, and therefore there must be in this colony a considerable number who had not been reached ; but it was gratifying to find that every year we were discovering them and bringing them here. There could not be a more striking proof of the interest which the ladies of Sydney took in the institution than the numbers in which they had assembled, notwithstanding the great and preternatural heat of the day. There was a striking difference between the deaf and dumb and the blind ; the former, from their peculiar disadvantages, could not be educated to the same high degree as the latter. They could be made to attain a high degree of proficiency in some of the mechanical arts ; they could be made good printers, book-binders, and so on—but if Mr. Watson could teach them to speak it would be an advantage. (A laugh.) He was not uttering a paradox in saying this, for the eminent Dr. Watson, who had devoted so much attention to this department of science, had affirmed that it was possible to do this—and there had been notable instances of people without tongues being, nevertheless, able to speak. There were two of the early martyrs instanced ; Gibbon sneered at this story, and it was at one time generally ascribed to miraculous intervention, but now parallel instances had been recorded. Dr. Syme had been called upon to cut out a man's tongue : and twelve months afterwards the patient had walked into his study, and asked him how he did. We are more dependent upon the ear than upon the tongue ; and by the wonderful art which some had acquired the deaf and dumb had been taught to speak. However, their education could not be carried very far. It was different with the blind ; they might be endowed with the genius of the poet, or the man of science, or the political power to accomplish mighty things. This had been proved in numerous cases, from "the blind old man in Scio's rocky isle, who sang to the music of the sea the Iliad and the Odyssey"—downwards. Another curious circumstance was that whilst in youthful years there were more deaf and dumb than blind, the blind out-numbered the deaf and dumb very rapidly, from the fact that many became blind at mature age, and a few were born blind. Of a thousand children born at a great institution in London, a scientific man who had attended there twenty-five years, had observed that not one was born blind. It had also been calculated that out of 1200 born deaf and dumb, not 700 arrived at 16 years of age, whereas it was common for the blind to live to be grey-haired. He hoped the general subscriptions would be a great deal larger next year, and would increase as the wants of the institution became more generally known. (Cheers.)

Mr. G. F. WISE seconded the resolution, which was put, and carried.

Rev. DANIEL ALLEN moved the next resolution :—" That the following gentlemen constitute the committee for the ensuing year :—President, the Rev. George King, M.A. ; vice-president, Rev. Dr. Lang ; hon. treasurer, Mr. Henry Philips ; hon. secretary, Mr. Ellis Robinson ; hon. surgeon, Mr. Arthur Renwick, M.D.; committee, Mr. E. T. Beilby, Mr. John Frazer, Mr. J. R. Fairfax, Mr. Robert Hills, Mr. James Henry, Rev. James Milne, Mr. William Love, J.P., Mr. William Rae, Mr. F. R. Robinson, Mr. George F. Wise, Mr. S. C. Brown, M.L.A., Mr. Alderman Linsley, J.P." By assisting our fellow creatures in affliction we followed in the footsteps of the greatest philanthropist that every lived, namely, Jesus Christ ; therefore, such services must be held in honour by us all. When he was a boy the lady teaching the highest class in the Sabbath school which he attended had been blind, and the circumstance had made a lasting impression upon him through life. He thought that an institution such as this, which could assist those afflicted as this lady was to read the Sacred Scriptures, must be worthy of our highest admiration and sympathies.

Rev. Mr. GALLOWAY seconded the resolution ; and it was passed without dissent.

Rev. G. KING proposed a vote of thanks to the Chairman, which was carried by acclamation, the company all rising.

The CHAIRMAN returned thanks.

The children were then examined. They all appeared healthy and contented. They were neatly clothed and clean, and had a well-fed cheery aspect, always pleasing to see in youth ; but upon the countenances of some, especially of the deaf and dumb, there was a restless and wandering expression somewhat painful to view. They appeared, however, by no means deficient in intelligence, and the attainments of those examined seemed very satisfactory. The commencement was the singing of a hymn, " Come, thou high and lofty Lord," by the blind children, accompanied on the harmonium by a little boy also blind. Then three of the blind children gave a pianoforte performance, consisting of selections from " Masaniello,"—played very creditably. The singing in chorus of the air " Spirit of the breeze " followed. Then two little girls read aloud, with much fluency, portions of the Scriptures printed in raised characters, so as to be traced by the hand. Their manipulation of these was truly marvellous. Neither of these poor children had been learning more than six or seven months, and it was an affecting sight to witness the manner in which they were enabled to acquire for themselves the words of life and consolation. They had been instructed by a pupil teacher, a blind young man, who had also been educated at the establishment.

The deaf and dumb were next examined in history and geography by means of questions written and answered upon the blackboard; the visitors being invited to examine for themselves. The proficiency displayed was really extremely creditable considering the age of the scholars and the affliction under which they suffered. The first question was, " Do you like this meeting ?" —to which a little girl readily answered " Yes." The next query (suggested by a visitor) was, " What is this meeting about ?" After a little difficulty another little girl responded, " The Annual Meeting." Then, " Do you know the chairman ?" was inscribed ; and " Mr. Hay" was the immediate response by a boy. To this succeeded the question, " When was Scotland annexed to England ?" to which were two responses "1306" and "1707," in the former case the pupil probably contemplating the subjugation by Edward III. The question, " In whose reign ?" was promptly answered " In the reign of Anne," by a little girl. Then the class were asked,—" When was Scotland first annexed to England ?" to which a female pupil replied at once " 1603." " Who was Anne," was then submitted, and answered—" The daughter of James II." by one little girl, another one further volunteering the character of the sovereign in question, which was to the effect that she was "a good quiet queen, possessed of many good qualities, but weak"—a brief epitome which created a good deal of amusement. " The Duke of Marlborough" was named as the celebrated general of Queen Anne's time ; and " Gibraltar," " Blenheim," " Oudinot," and "Saragossa" suggested as a few of his victories. One of the boys, however, intimated that it was Sir George Rooke who captured Gibraltar. The question " Who was the best Queen of England ?" was, of course, promptly answered " Victoria ;" but upon the point who was the best queen leaving the reigning sovereign out of consideration, there was a difference of opinion, one child suggesting " Mary II.," and another " Elizabeth." There was also much variance as to who was " the best King of England"—a question which after all might puzzle much more experienced and deeply read scholars. " Edward III.," " William III.," and " Alfred" were submitted. The reign of Queen Elizabeth was stated at thirty-seven and forty-four years.

Mr. ELLIS ROBINSON read a letter which he had received from a former deaf and dumb inmate of the institution who had been taken home to Brisbane. He spoke in terms of affection both of the asylum, its teachers and friends, and the old pupils; referring to many of the latter by name, and mixing up, whimsically enough, inquiries after their health and well-being, with hopes that their arithmetical acquirements were in a fair way. The letter was a well-written one ; and though the production of a deaf and dumb boy who, four years ago was altogether ignorant, it would bear very favourable comparison with the productions of many of the most efficient boys in our public schools.

A dialogue between a blind boy and a deaf and dumb boy created a good deal of interest. This was accomplished by the former conversing upon the fingers of the latter—who replied in the same way. The blind boy was desired to ask different questions of his deaf and dumb friend ; they were at once responded to, and the blind boy (a smart lively little fellow) apprised the audience of the answers. His brightness of manner created some amusement. He was requested to ask where the Governor was, and he shortly afterwards informed the company that the answer was " in Fiji." " Now," added he, " I'll ask him where Fiji is." This appeared rather a poser for the little deaf-mute ; but after a minute or two his friend, with an expression of some pity for the other's geographical shortcomings, said, " I suppose he means in the Pacific."

Two blind boys then recited Longfellow's "Psalm of Life," and "Sound the loud timbral o'er Egypt's dark sea," respectively ; and two deaf-and-dumb boys illustrated the same in pantomime.

This closed the examination, and the company dispersed to view the building, &c. The most recent alteration since our last notice is the erection of two very fine cedar tablets in the entrance hall, with the names of the "life directors" on one, and those of the givers of donations or bequests of above £50* on the other. The lettering is in gold, with illuminated capitals and ornamental scrolls, and the general effect is harmonious and neat. The boards are from Hudson, Brothers, Redfern ; the lettering by Mr. A. R. Pullin, of Park-street.

The pleased and contented appearance of the children could not fail to strike every one who saw them. Many of the deaf and dumb children are pretty and very intelligent looking ; and a close and affectionate companionship seemed to exist between them and their fellow-afflicted ones, the blind. They were all neatly and nicely dressed, not with the odious uniformity common to charitable institutions, but in ordinary garments, with no regard to resemblance ; and this circumstance seemed to make them appear happier looking, and more like the members of one family than the inmates of an asylum. After the examination, several of the ladies present visited the institution, in order to inspect the arrangements and observe its management.

Sydney, 30th September, 1874.

HENRY PHILLIPS, *Hon. Treasurer*, in a/c with N. S. W. Institution for the Deaf & Dumb, & the Blind.

Dr. GENERAL FUND ACCOUNT. **Cr.**

INCOME.

	£	s.	d.
To Balance at credit of last year's account......	111	16	6
,, Subscriptions and Donations (public).........	867	7	7
,, Annual Grant from New South Wales Government	450	0	0
,, Amount received for School Fees and Clothing collected by Mr. W. G. O'Neil, Queanbeyan	333	10	3
,, collected by Mr. H. Churchill, Port Macquarie	40	1	0
,, received for Verdict District Court, Yeates v. Davis, per Mr. C. S. Jones, Solicitor	15	10	0
,, received for surplus funds, Mayor's Picnic, per Messrs. Spence and Smart	2	2	0
,, received from contribution boxes at the Institution, £3 10s., £3 9s. 9d...	7	0	0
	6	19	9
	£1,834	**7**	**1**

To Balance brought down being at credit in Commercial Bank £209 12 10

Audited and found correct,

EDWIN T. BEILBY, } *Auditors.*
WILLIAM LOVE.

EXPENDITURE.

	£	s.	d.
By Salaries	536	12	4
,, Provisions, Groceries, &c.	461	12	11
,, Furniture, Additions, Repairs, &c.	167	18	7
,, Drapery, Clothing, Boots, &c.	123	8	7
,, Fuel, Lighting, and Medicine	65	11	6
,, Advertising, Printing, Stationery, and Printing Annual Reports......	88	10	7
,, Sundries, Petty House Expenses, &c.	98	8	8
,, Commission, Collecting Expenses, Stamps, &c.	67	10	11
,, Interest paid to Bank on overdrawn account...	5	5	2
,, Remitted to England for Books for the Blind...	5	0	0
,, Insurance of Buildings and Furniture	4	15	0
,, Balance, being amount at credit in Commercial Bank	209	12	10
	£1,834	**7**	**1**

E. & O. E.

Sydney, 30th September, 1874.

HENRY PHILLIPS, *Hon. Treasurer.*

Sydney, 30th September, 1874.

HENRY PHILLIPS, *Hon. Treasurer, in a/c with* N. S. W. INSTITUTION FOR THE DEAF & DUMB, & THE BLIND.

BUILDING FUND ACCOUNT.

Dr.

INCOME.

	£	s.	d.
To Balance at credit in Commercial Bank as per last year's account	674	9	3
" Sundry Donations from the Public	19	1	0
" Proportion of Exhibition Fancy Fair, per Mr. W. B. Campbell	54	15	7
" Bequest of the late Maurice Alexander	50	0	0
" " Hamilton Hunne	50	0	0
" " William Moffitt	250	0	0
" Amount of collections by Mr. C. W. Newman, Aralucn	1	7	0
" " Mr. W. Davis, Little River	2	9	3
" " Mr. Luff, in Country Districts by as per lists in Report	461	17	0
	£1,563	19	1

	£	s.	d.
To Balance brought down, being amount in Commercial Bank	£330	17	10

Audited and found correct,

EDWIN T. BEILBY, } *Auditors.*
WILLIAM LOVE. }

Cr.

EXPENDITURE.

	£	s.	d.
By Payment to Contractor for erection of new Verandahs, Fuel House, &c.	1012	16	9
" Commission to Architect on ditto	50	12	6
" Interest paid Bank on overdrawn account	3	17	3
" Commission on Country collections, Advertising, Travelling, and other expenses	165	14	9
" Balance carried down, being amount at credit in Commercial Bank	330	17	10
	£1,563	19	1

E. & O. E.

Sydney, 30th September, 1874.

HENRY PHILLIPS, *Hon. Treasurer.*

NOTE.—Of this Balance of £330 17s. 10d., a sum of about £150 is now being expended in making the carriage road and guttering it.

Annual Subscriptions, Donations, &c.

Received for the Year ending 30th September, 1874.

— oo —

☞ N.B.—It is particularly requested that any omission or inaccuracy in this list be notified to the Secretary for correction.

	£	s.	d.		£	s.	d.
2228.	2	2	0	Button, C. Maitland... ...	2	0	0
A Friend	0	2	6	Baass, J. C. H....	1	1	0
A Friend	0	5	0	Blunt, G. Muswellbrook...	1	1	0
A Friend, Newtown... ...	0	5	0	Briggs, W. Maitland ...	1	1	0
Alexander, Mrs.	1	1	0	Blair, R. Maitland	1	0	0
Anonymous, ½ £1 note ...	0	10	0	Bawden, T., M.L.A. Grafton	1	1	0
Allt and Co.	1	1	0	Brentnall, A. G. Yass ...	1	1	0
Allan, H. Edward A. ...	1	1	0	Broadhurst, Mrs.	1	1	0
Allwood, Rev. Canon ...	1	1	0	Bellew, Mrs. Piercefield ...	1	1	0
Abbey, W....	1	1	0	Brown, H. J. Newcastle...	1	1	0
Adam, John S....	2	2	0	Blaldwin, C. Maitland ...	2	2	0
Atherden, Mrs. Donation	5	0	0	Brownhill, James, Grafton	0	10	0
Aiken, T.	1	0	0	Beyers, H. L. Hill End ...	1	0	0
Alger, J.	1	1	0	Baylis, E.	0	10	0
Alderson and Sons	1	1	0	Butler, W., Brisbane ...	1	1	0
Adams, Mrs., Newtown ...	0	5	0	Butler, Mrs., ditto	1	1	0
Allen, Hon. G., M.L.C. ...	5	0	0	Beit, H.	1	1	0
Anderson, James	0	10	0	Biss, Mrs. H., quarterly...	0	5	0
Antrobus, J.	0	10	0	Brocklehurst, W. W., per			
Anderson and Hall	1	1	0	W. Wolfen & Co.... ...	5	0	0
Ariell, W. H.	1	1	0	Barnard and Hinton ...	1	1	0
Allen, John	0	10	6	Buck, R., Newtown... ...	0	5	0
Adams, Rev. F. W. Pater-				Binnie, R....	1	1	0
son...	0	10	0	Bradley, Newton, & Lamb	1	1	0
Anonymous, Denman ...	1	0	0	Buchanan, B.	2	2	0
Anonymous, Wagga ...	0	10	0	Bull, Henry	1	1	0
Ash, F., Newcastle	1	0	0	Baillie, Mrs. J. H.	1	0	0
Anonymous, Scone	0	10	0	Begg, John E....	1	1	0
Ash, William, Singleton ...	1	1	0	Bell, H.	1	1	0
Abbott, Mrs., Dungog ...	1	0	0	Brown and Co....	1	1	0
Anonymous, Grafton ...	0	10	0	Bennett, S., *Empire*... ...	1	1	0
Armstrong, W., Inverell...	0	10	0	Buzacott and Armstrong...	1	1	0
Asser, F., Scone	0	10	0	Bull, W.	1	1	0
Allen, D. T., Newcastle ...	0	10	0	Brush, J.	1	1	0

	£	s.	d.
Brereton, Dr. Le Gay ...	2	2	0
Blackburn and Co.	1	1	0
Booth, Mrs. Balmain ...	0	15	0
Bird, H. S.	1	1	0
Barker, W.	2	2	0
Bates, Miss Emma	2	0	0
Boucher, J., Cooma ...	1	1	0
Barker, T. Hon. M.L.C., Maryland	2	0	0
Biss, Mrs. H.	0	5	0
Beilby and Scott	1	1	0
Bennett, Dr.	1	1	0
Breillat, Mrs.	1	0	0
Buchanan, W....	1	1	0
Brown, S. C. M.L.A. ...	2	2	0
Brewster, John...	2	2	0
Bown, Charles...	1	1	0
Barker, Right Rev. Dr. Bishop	2	2	0
Biddell, Brothers	1	1	0
Baker, Thomas...	1	1	0
Busby, Hon. W., M.L.C....	2	2	0
Cooke, Mrs.	0	5	0
Contribution Boxes, Visitors	6	19	9
Churchill, Mr. H., Dungog Creek, Port McQuarie,			
Collected by—			
Wilson, T. G., Rollands Plains	1	0	0
Dangar, O. O.	0	10	6
Tingcombe, G., Rollands Plains	0	10	0
Kemp, R. A. H., Salmons Plains	0	10	0
King, A.	0	10	0
Stanley, A.	0	10	0
Stewart, Mrs. J., Rowlands	0	5	0
Webster, John, Wilson River	0	5	0
Farrawell, Mrs., Wilson River	0	5	0
Halliday, George, Wilson River	0	5	0
Doyle, John, Rollands Plains	0	5	0
Scott, G. T. Millin ...	0	5	0
Jason, Kempsey ...	0	5	0
Dangar, W. T. Kempsey	0	5	0
Poole, W. S. Hampden Hall	0	5	0

	£	s.	d.
Gildon, G. P.M. Kempsey	0	5	0
Smith, F. Kempsey ...	0	5	0
Lyon, John, Kempsey...	0	5	0
Sums under 5s.	8	19	6
Critchley, Mrs., Darling Point	10	0	0
Carey, Cohen and Gilles	1	1	0
Cortis, Dr., Bathurst ...	1	1	0
Charles White's penny box	1	13	11
Callaghan and Son	1	1	0
Cracknell, E. C.	1	1	0
Chisholm, Mrs.	5	5	0
Crane, W., J.P.	1	1	0
Cowlishaw Brothers ...	1	1	0
Chadwick, R.	1	1	0
Cox, Hon. G. H., M.L.C.	2	2	0
Cohen Brothers	1	1	0
Cooper, Nathan and Co. ...	1	1	0
Carmichael, J....	0	5	0
Caird, Paterson and Co. ...	1	0	0
Campbell, Hon. C., M.L.C.	2	2	0
Campbell, Hon. John, M.L.C.	2	2	0
Campbell, J. W., Singleton	1	0	0
Cooke, H. H., Parkes ...	1	1	0
Carss, W.	1	0	0
Campbell, Allan, Yass ...	2	0	0
Carraher, O. J., J.P. ...	1	1	0
Campbell, M., Muswellbrook	1	1	0
Capper and Sons, West Maitland	1	1	0
Cowper, Very Rev. Dean	1	0	0
Church, W.	1	1	0
Challacombe, N., Cowra ...	1	0	0
Campbell, Hon. A., M.L.C.	1	1	0
Cox, J. H., Nogon	1	1	0
Cohen, H. E.	0	10	6
Crane, Mrs., per J. B. Allpress...	1	1	0
Copas, George, The late, per T. Spence and E. Carter, Executors ...	25	0	0
C. P....	0	5	0
Carr, H. C., Fanny Hill, Binda	0	10	0
Crowley, W., J.P., Cobbedah	0	10	0
Child, Rev. Canon, Morpeth	0	10	6
Cotter, W. A., Wagga Wagga	1	1	0
Creer, E., Grafton	0	10	0

	£	s.	d.
Capel, D., J.P., Piedmont, Barrabu, ... £1	1	0	0
Collected by—			
Burrett, W.	0	2	6
Bird, G.	0	2	6
Hogg, T.	0	2	6
Quin, P.	0	2	6
Selslow	0	5	0
Erapes, E.	0	5	0
Bingford, H.	0	2	6
Burnett, W.	0	2	6
Hewitt	0	2	6
Murray, W.	0	2	6
Grant, J.	0	2	6
Ah Hew	0	2	6
Capel, Annie	0	1	0
Page, G., junr.	0	1	0
Clarke, Janet	0	3	0
	3	0	0
Cram, P., Young	1	0	0
Darley, Hon. F. M., M.L.C.	1	1	0
Dibbs, T. A.	2	2	0
Donald, Rev. W. S. ...	1	1	0
Durham, T., Singleton ...	1	1	0
Dixson and Son	1	1	0
Dangar, F. H.	30	0	0
Davis, W., Little River, collected by	0	7	6
Davis, J., Kiandra House	0	5	0
Dangar, H. C.	3	3	0
Dangar, Mrs. H. C.	1	1	0
Davis, D. A.	0	10	0
Deane, J. L.	1	1	0
Donnithorne, Miss	1	1	0
Dight, Mrs., Richmond, per Mrs. Hay	1	0	0
Davidson, W.	0	10	0
Dempsey, M. J.	1	1	0
Daintry, E.	1	1	0
Dale, W., J.P., Orange ...	0	10	0
Durham, G.	2	2	0
Dalley, W. B.	1	1	0
Dearin, T. B.	1	1	0
DeLissa, S.	1	1	0
Day, Mrs., senr.	1	0	0
Dunsmure, Mrs.	1	0	0
Dangar, A. A., "Baroona"	3	3	0
Dangar, W. J.	2	2	0
Dibbs, John C., Newcastle	1	1	0
Dangar, W. C., "Osterley"	1	1	0
Doyle, J. F. & G. "Kaloudah"	1	0	0
Davis, John, Grafton ...	1	0	0
Drummond, J. & M., Bookham	1	0	0
Day, W., J.P.	1	0	0
Evans, W. T. C.P.S., Orange, per G. F. Wise	1	1	0
Ellis, Donation	0	10	8
England, Mr., Traupa Station, Queensland, per Mrs. Allison	1	0	0
Elouis, C.	5	0	0
Elliott, P. J. and Co., ...	1	1	0
Exhibition Fancy Fair, per W. B. Campbell ...	54	15	7
E. J.	1	0	0
Evans, Captain, J.P. ...	1	1	0
Elrie, Mrs. per Mrs. Blundell, Donation ...	2	0	0
Farmer Messrs. and Company	1	1	0
Farmer, Mrs.	1	0	0
Farquhar, Capt. A. B. ...	0	10	6
Fache, C. J.	3	0	0
Flower, Miss, per Mrs. Allwood	1	0	0
Francis, A. Surveyor, near Bathurst	2	0	0
Fairclough, Capt. H. ...	2	2	0
Fraser, Mrs., Brisbane Water	1	0	0
Forster, Miss, Ryde	1	0	0
Fell, J. W. per Mrs. Goodlet	1	0	0
Friend, W. S.	2	2	0
Ford, R. T.	1	1	0
Forsyth, A.	3	3	0
Ford, R. T., 2nd sub. ...	1	1	0
Faucett, Justice	1	1	0
Frank, J. P.	0	10	6
Frazer, J. and Co.	2	2	0
Fairfax, John	1	1	0
Fairfax, J. R.	1	1	0
Fairfax, E. R.	1	1	0
Fanning, Griffiths and Co.	2	0	0
Foster, R.	0	10	0
Frazer, Hon. John, M.L.C.	5	5	0
Fox, Captain Henry T. ...	1	1	0
Flavelle, Brothers & Roberts	1	1	0
Ferguson, G.	1	1	0
Fletcher, John J.P., Walcha	2	0	0
Frankland, G. J., J.P. Paterson	1	0	0
Fache, C. J.	2	2	0

	£	s.	d.
Fenwick, C. D. J.P. "Europampbela"	1	0	0
Freeman, W. " Greeuwich "	1	0	0
Fairfax, Mrs. Charles ...	2	2	0
Fitzpatrick, M., M.L.A. ...	1	0	0
Finch, John, Maitland ...	1	0	0
Faunce, Rev. A. D., Bega	0	10	0
Forsyth, George, Wagga Wagga	1	1	0
Geekie, Rev. Dr. Bathurst	1	1	0
Glasson, Richard, J.P., Guyong...	1	0	0
Gibson, H. S.	0	10	6
Gregson, S.	1	0	0
Gibson, J. J., Reedy Creek per Mrs. John Hay ...	4	0	0
Gardiner, W. and S. ...	1	1	0
Greenhill, S.	2	2	0
Gilchrist and Weston ...	1	1	0
Gray, Miss	1	0	0
Gill, John, J.P.'Gostwyck'	1	0	0
Gibson, G. L., Longford...	1	0	0
Gully, W., Highert... ...	1	0	0
Gennys, Capt. J. H., J.P., "Stoke"	1	0	0
Graham, John	1	1	0
Gravemaker, E., Grenfell	1	0	0
Gardiner, John, Wallabadah	1	0	0
Holle, J. F.	1	1	0
H. and M. Donation ...	0	15	6
Hillier, Mrs. per J. Henry	1	0	0
Hassall, Mrs.	1	0	0
Harris, W. Collected by, Wollombi	4	0	0
H. J. P.	0	5	0
Hemsley, C.	0	10	6
Hobson, Mrs.	1	0	0
Heazy, per W. B. Campbell	0	10	0
Howard, W. Balmain ...	0	10	0
Hinchcliffe, A....	1	1	0
Howe, Mrs. A....	1	0	0
Harrison and Attwood ...	1	1	0
Harrison, J. S....	1	1	0
Hay, Hon. J., M.L.C. ...	2	0	0
Hordern, L. and E.... ...	2	2	0
Hudson Brothers	1	1	0
Hoffnung and Co.	1	1	0
Huchinson, D. B.	2	2	0
Holdsworth, J. B.	2	2	0

	£	s.	d.
Humphrey, F. T.	1	1	0
Hanks, J. G. and Co. ...	1	1	0
Hills, R.	2	2	0
Holdsworth, R.	1	1	0
Holt, Hon. T., M.L.C. ...	5	0	0
Hay, Hon. John, M.L.C....	5	0	0
Hargrave, R. J.P., Hill Grove	1	0	0
Hamburger Brothers ...	2	2	0
Hart, S. West Maitland...	1	1	0
Horne, S. H., Singleton ...	1	0	0
Hardy Brothers, Hunter Street	1	1	0
Haslingden, G. Bega ...	1	1	0
Harris, Richard, Newcastle	1	0	0
Hargrave, E. J.P. Hernani	1	0	0
Hume, A. H. Everton Donation	2	2	0
Harnett, Mrs. Mary Eucumbene	1	0	0
Harrison, J. S....	1	1	0
Hall, G. P. Blairmore ...	1	0	0
Hill, Mrs. W. C. Donation per Captain Smith ...	5	0	0
Hordern, A.	2	2	0
Henry, J....	2	2	0
Harrison, L. M.	1	1	0
I.O.O.F.M.U., per A. Kethel, Donation	5	5	0
Isaacs, J. & Co.	2	2	0
Irving, D. W., P.M., Tamworth	1	0	0
Innes, T., Newcastle ...	1	1	0
Ireland, J., ditto	0	10	0
Isaac, F., Scone	0	10	0
Jaques, C. E., J.P., Morpeth	0	10	0
Jones, R., "Stoneleigh "...	1	1	0
Jillings, F., Newcastle ...	1	0	0
Jolly, W., J.P....	1	1	0
Jacques, T. J.	1	0	0
Jenkins, Dr., J.P., Nepean Towers	5	0	0
Jeffers, Miss	0	10	6
Jones, D. and Co.	2	2	0
Jones, Dr. P., Sydney ...	1	1	0
Johnson, Rev. Thomas ...	1	0	0
J. C.	0	5	0
Josephson, Judge, per J. G. Raphael, M.L.A.	2	2	0
Jones, Stephen W.	1	1	0

	£	s.	d.		£	s.	d.
J. L.	1	1	0	Macgregor, James	1	1	0
Jones, T. T. and Son ...	1	1	0	Moore, Mrs. R. W., North			
Jones, E., Cadow	0	10	0	Shore	1	1	0
Johnston, W., Clarence				Moore, Dr. W....	1	0	0
Town	1	1	0	Mullens, Mrs., Balmain...	0	10	0
Jardine, W., Curry Flat,				Murray, J., ditto	0	10	0
Cooma	1	1	0	Morehead, R. A. A.... ...	2	2	0
				Montefiore, Joseph & Co.	1	1	0
Kent, Mrs., "Euston," Too-				Moore, C., M.L.A.	2	2	0
woomba, Queensland,				Manning, Hon. Sir W.,			
per Mrs. Hay	10	10	0	M.L.C.	1	1	0
King, G. and Co.	1	1	0	Miller, R....	0	10	6
Keep and Parsons	1	1	0	Myers, J. H.	0	10	6
Kelk and Alford	1	0	0	Maxwell, A. C..., ...	1	1	0
Knox, E.	2	2	0	Mansfield, G. A.	1	1	0
Keep, J.	1	1	0	Myers and Solomon... ...	2	2	0
Kinsela, C...	1	1	0	Moore, Alexander & Co....	1	1	0
Knaggs, R. C., Newcastle	0	10	0	Mills, J.	1	1	0
Kesterton, H., J.P., Bom-				Macpherson, E. A.... ...	1	1	0
bala	1	0	0	Macpherson, Joseph ...	1	1	0
King, Rev. George, M.A...	1	0	0	Manning, Charles J. ...	1	1	0
				Manson, J. Forbes	1	1	0
Lenehan, Mrs. H. A. ...	1	1	0	Macintyre, Mrs. "Kayuja"	1	0	0
Levick, James	1	1	0	Mackenzie, J. P.	1	1	0
Lane, J. B., J.P., Orange	1	1	0	Marse, W. H. J.P. "Abing-			
Langley, Rev. H. A. Bal-				ton...	1	1	0
main	1	1	0	Montague, A. J.P. Cooma	1	0	0
Lester, Miss	1	0	0	Mitchell, George, Newcastle	1	0	0
Lassetter, F. and Co. ...	1	1	0	Mitchell, G. Washington			
Leathes, A. S.	2	2	0	ditto, Donation	0	8	8
Lorimer, Marwood & Rome	1	1	0	Mitchell, Miss Louisa, ditto			
Laidley, W. and Co... ...	2	2	0	ditto	0	3	4
Lamb, Mrs.	1	1	0	May, J. M.	1	1	0
Lord, E.	1	0	0	Mort, Henry	2	2	0
Levey, Montague, J.P. ...	1	1	0	Moore, James, Singleton ..	1	1	0
Leibus, Dr.	1	1	0	Miller, M., Scone	0	10	0
Linsley, J. R., Alderman...	1	1	0	Meillon, J., Grafton... ...	0	10	0
Lord, Mrs. F.	0	10	6	Mort, T. S.	3	3	0
Levy, L. W., M.L.A. ...	2	2	0	McCoy Brothers	1	1	0
Lawson, Miss, Dr. Beg's				McCabe, F. P., J.P.,			
Bible Class, Collected at	0	15	0	Wollongong	1	1	0
Lesley, W. C., Singleton...	1	1	0	McDonnell, W.	1	0	0
Lockhead, W. K., Newcastle	1	1	0	McDonald, R., Donation...	0	6	0
Lawson, G. Yass	0	10	0	McDonald, Smith and Co.	2	2	0
Love, J. R.	1	1	0	McArthur, A., and Co. ...	2	2	0
Lewis, Brothers, Tamworth	1	1	0	McCulloch, T.	1	1	0
Loyal Orange Lodge No.				McQuade, Mrs.	1	1	0
37, per Mr. McCoy ...	2	2	0	McDougall, "Lorn," West			
				Maitland	1	0	0
Mitchell, J. S.	1	0	0	McKeachie, A., Delegate...	1	0	0
Monro, James	0	10	0	McDonall, J., J.P., "New			
Milne, Rev. James, M.A.				Frough"	0	10	0
(1873)	1	0	0	McFadden, H., Singleton	0	10	6
Metcalfe, Mrs.	1	1	0				

	£	s.	d.		£	s.	d.
Nemo, per G. F. Wise ...	1	1	0	Piercy, Thomas, Parkes ...	0	10	0
Neale, J. H., M.L.A. ...	1	1	0	Potts, W. E., Murrurundi	0	10	0
Norton, J.	1	1	0	Parrett, J. "Tyringham"			
Nichol, D....	1	0	0	S. Grafton	1	0	0
Noake, J.	0	10	0				
Nicholson, J., Glen View,				Raymond, R., Peel	2	0	0
Grange, Bombala... ...	1	1	0	Russell, H. C.	1	0	0
Nainby, F., Morpeth ...	0	10	6	Reddie, Mrs., Millers			
Newman, J., Gunning ...	1	0	0	Point, per Ramsay ...	1	0	0
Naylor, J., Bega	0	10	0	Robinson, G. L., Windsor	1	1	0
Newton, E., J.P., Burraba	1	0	0	Riley, W. R., Goulburn			
Nicholl, Mrs., Scone ...	0	5	0	Donation	0	15	0
O'Hare, J. "Corrowong"	0	10	0	Ranken, Mrs., Newtown...	0	5	0
Shinfield, J. ditto ...	0	5	0	Rush, James, Orange ...	1	0	0
Garrett, E. ditto ...	0	5	0	Robinson, His Excellency			
O'Brien, Mr., Grenfell ...	1	1	0	Sir Hercules, K.C.B. &c.	3	0	0
Old, R. North Shore ...	2	0	0	Raphael, J. G. M.L.A· ...	1	1	0
Osborne, Miss, per F. B.				Ross, J. Grafton	1	1	0
McCabe, J.P.	5	0	0	Roach, W. R.	1	1	0
Oakes, George M.L.A. ...	1	1	0	Ross, Morgan and Co. ...	2	2	0
O'Brien, Kerridge, and				Richardson and Wrench...	1	1	0
McKay	1	1	0	Raynes, E...	1	1	0
Ogilvie, Mrs. Mary... ...	1	1	0	Rhodes, B.	0	5	0
Osborne, James	1	1	0	Rabone, Feez and Co. ...	1	1	0
Oriental Banking Company, per S. Murray ...	5	5	0	Reeve, T. P.	1	0	0
Oatley, Mrs. F.	1	0	0	Ralston, A. J.	1	1	0
Owen, W....	1	1	0	Ryrie, A. and D. "Coolringdon"	5	0	0
Osborne, H.	2	0	0	Reading, E.	1	1	0
				Ryan, E. W. J.P., South			
Pemell, James and Co. ...	1	1	0	Grafton	1	0	0
Perkins, Thomas	1	1	0	Robinson, ...	0	10	0
Prince, Ogg and Co.... ...	1	1	0	Russell, P. N. and Co. ...	1	1	0
Peapes and Shaw	1	1	0	Ryrie, S., Cooma	1	0	0
Perry, William and Co. ...	1	1	0	Reid, John, Newcastle ...	1	1	0
Penfold, E. T. J.P.	3	3	0	Rae, William	2	0	0
Peate and Harcourt... ...	2	2	0	Randell, Captain	3	3	0
Powell, Mrs. George ...	1	1	0	Rowe, W. M., Newcastle...	0	10	0
Phillips, J. O., Bathurst...	1	1	0	Reynolds, A. Seymour ...	0	10	0
Perkins, Thomas, Balmain	1	1	0	Robinson, F. R.	1	1	0
Pratt, J. C.	0	5	0				
Parbury, Lamb and Co. ...	1	1	0				
Palser, H. P. J.P.	0	10	0	Sun Kum On	0	10	6
Plummer, J. G.	0	10	0	Senior, F.	1	1	0
Perks, F.	1	1	0	Surplus Fund Mayor's Picnic, One-third, per			
Pitt, G. M.	1	1	0	Spence and Smart J.P's.	7	0	0
Potts, Mrs.	3	0	0	St. Stephen's Presbyterian			
Pyne, D., J.P., Grenfell...	1	1	0	Church	2	0	0
Price, W.	1	1	0	Smith, W....	1	0	0
Pring, James, Ashfield ...	1	0	0	Stubbs, R. F., and Co. ...	2	2	0
Phillips, Henry	1	1	0	Sands, John	1	1	0
Peberdy, Thomas, Tenterfield	1	1	0	Smart, Hon. T. W., M.L.C.	1	1	0

Smith, James, J.P., "Llan-arth," Bathurst	£1	1	0	
Samuel, Hon. S., M.L.C....	1	1	0	
Saddington, Alfred	2	2	0	
Stewart, Garrick and Co.	1	1	0	
Smith, F. J., Toojong ...	0	10	0	
Smith, F., ditto	0	10	0	
Sutton, A. W., J.P.... ...	1	1	0	
Smith, Professor	1	1	0	
Stephen and Stephen ...	1	1	0	
Starkey, J.	1	1	0	
Stevens, C. J.	1	1	0	
Stutchbury, T. J.	1	1	0	
Staff, J. F., per C. H. Humphrey	1	0	0	
Sinclair, Captain, P.M., Grafton...	1	0	0	
Stevens, R., ditto	1	1	0	
Selman, D. B., ditto... ...	1	0	0	
Skarratt, C. C.	1	1	0	
Strickland, Josiah, Forbes	1	1	0	
Smith, R. B., M.L.A. ...	1	1	0	
Sly, J.	1	1	0	
Stiles, C., J.P. "Kanoona"	1	0	0	
Sippel, J., Grenfell... ...	0	5	0	
Spasshatt, Dr., Armidale...	1	0	0	
Smith, Shepherd	2	2	0	
Smith, Shepherd, pro Bank N. S. W. Donation ...	10	0	0	
Stewart, Rev. C.	1	0	0	
Spencer, Walter W.... ...	1	0	0	
Scholes, J., senr., Armidale	0	10	0	
Shultz, John, Eden	1	0	0	
Scott, Captain, P.M. ...	1	1	0	
Saunder, J. M., West Maitland	1	0	0	
Saxby, H., Gunning ...	1	0	0	
Sharpe, J. B.	1	0	0	
Selfe, N.	0	10	0	
Stephen, M. H....	3	0	0	
Simpson, W. H.	1	1	0	
Street, Norton and Co. ...	1	1	0	
Salomons, J. E.	1	1	0	
Sim, R.	1	0	0	
Smail, James	0	10	6	
Scott, D.	1	1	0	
Spring, James	1	1	0	
Speer, W., J.P.	1	1	0	
Skinner, T. and J.	1	1	0	
Stanley, Rev. Dr.	1	1	0	
Smyth and Wells	0	10	0	
Saber, W....	1	1	0	
Tooth, Messrs., and Co. ...	2	2	0	
Thompson & Giles, Messrs.	2	2	0	

Trebeck, Mr. and Mrs. ...	£1	1	0	
Thomas, T. Marrickville...	2	2	0	
Taylor, Rev. R.	1	0	0	
Taylor, Mr. Newtown, per Mr. Mills	1	0	0	
Taylor, Ernest, Tamworth	1	0	0	
Trickett, W. J....	1	1	0	
Thompson, R.	0	10	0	
Tickle, J. B.	1	1	0	
Towns, R., Messrs., and Co.	2	2	0	
Teakle, C.	1	1	0	
Thomson, E. Deas, Hon., M.L.C....	1	1	0	
Terry, R. R.	1	1	0	
Thorne, Mrs.	2	2	0	
Thompson, A. J.P.	1	1	0	
Thomas, Messrs. A. W., Forbes	1	1	0	
Tasmanian Government ...	14	0	0	
Thurlow, C. A....	1	1	0	
Taylor, Mrs., "Terrible Vale"	1	1	0	
Talbot, Messrs., and Son...	2	2	0	
Thompson, Joseph	1	1	0	
Teale, Mrs.	1	1	0	
Turner, J....	0	10	0	
Tighe, A. A. P., Newcastle	1	0	0	
Thomas, Mrs. F. J.	1	0	0	
Thomson, W., Bega ...	0	10	0	
Tucker, Messrs., and Co....	1	1	0	
Uther, W.	3	0	0	
Verdict in Yeates v. Davies District Court, per Mr. C. S. Jones, Solicitor ...	2	2	0	
Vickery, E.	2	0	0	
Vallack, W.	1	0	0	
Verey, H. & J., Messrs ...	1	1	0	
Vernon, J., Scone	3	0	0	
Voss, Houlton H., Union Club	2	2	0	
Wyndham, Alexander, "Winton" Goondiwindy Queensland	1	0	0	
Watts, George	2	0	0	
Wade, J., Dungog	1	1	0	
Wilson, W. J., Newtown	1	0	0	
West, George, Newtown...	0	10	0	
Walker, Thomas, Concord	10	0	0	
Wood, J. B., per S. Watson...	1	0	0	
White, F. R.	1	0	0	
Want, R. C.	1	1	0	

	£	s.	d.		£	s.	d.
Woolnough, H. and Co. ...	1	1	0	Wingate, Mrs.	1	1	0
Woolcot, W. P.	0	10	6	Woods Brothers, Now-			
Way, E.	1	1	0	castle	1	1	0
Wearne, Joseph, M.L.A.	1	1	0	Whorcat, E. R. Tenterfield	1	1	0
Wright, J. M.	1	1	0	Watson Brothers, Matong	2	2	0
Walford and Sparke ...	1	1	0	White, Mrs. Senr., Mus-			
Wood, J.	0	10	6	wellbrook	2	2	0
Woolley, Mrs.	0	10	0				
Warburton and Co.	1	1	0	Young & Lark...	1	1	0
West, T. H. M.L.A.,				Young, J., South Creck,			
Carcoar...	0	10	0	per Rev. W. Ridley ...	5	0	0
Wolfe and Gorrick, West				Yates, L., C.P.S, Yass ...	1	1	0
Maitland	1	0	0				
White, James J.P.,							
Martindale	1	0	0	Zions, H.	1	1	0
Wyndham, John, Dalwood	2	2	0	Zollner, S....	0	10	0

SUPPLEMENTARY LIST.

	£	s.	d.		£	s.	d.
Alexander, Mrs., per G. F.				Payne, R., Grafton	£1	0	0
Wise	£1	1	0				
Anderson, J., Maitland ...	0	10	0	Renwick, Dr.	2	2	0
Biss, Mrs., (quarterly sub-				Renwick, G.	1	1	0
scription	0	5	0	Robinson, Mrs. G. L.,			
Cook, Messrs. Joseph & Co.	0	10	6	Windsor	1	1	0
Dight, Mrs. E. M., Staf-				Smyth, S. H.	2	2	0
ford, Singleton	1	0	0				
Farnell, Hon. James S. ...	1	0	0	Wearing, B. C.	1	0	0
Gay, E., Tamworth	0	10	0	Wise, G. F.	1	1	0
Goldsworthy, Mrs., (School				*Per Mr. J. Stames :—*			
Fee)	2	10	0	Stames, John	1	1	0
Gill, John, J.P.,"Moonby"	1	0	0	R. W. C....	0	10	0
Hand, Frederick, Bega ...	1	0	0	Davis, B.	0	2	0
				Dunn, Andrew...	0	5	0
Metcalfe, Mrs.	1	1	0	Abraham, S.	0	2	6
Mitchell, George, New-				Tanor, T.	0	10	0
castle	1	0	0	McAlister, L.	0	2	0
M. N.	1	0	0	Nevill, J.	0	2	6
Milne, Rev. J....	1	1	0	Perbert, R.	0	2	6
				White, A....	0	2	6
Polding, His Grace Arch-				Harris, A.	0	2	6
bishop	1	1	0	Armstrong, —	0	5	0

Country Collections.

NEW SOUTH WALES.

Per Mr. GEORGE LUFF.

* Donations under 5s. are placed in Lump Sums.

ARALUEN.

	£	s.	d.
Earl, Rev. R. T.	0	10	0
Burnell, T. C.	0	10	0
Smith, E.	0	10	0
Larcombe, E.	0	5	0
Walton, L.	0	5	0
Hobbs, Mrs.	0	5	0
Grimshaw, J.	0	10	0
Heeger, C....	0	5	0
Burne, H. P.M.	0	10	0
Lyons, Rev. Father W. ...	0	10	0
Carlisle, E. F.	0	5	0
Price, H.	0	10	0
Sneddon, A.	0	5	0
Johnson, W. H.	0	10	0
Wa Kee	0	5	0
Newman, C. W.	0	5	0
Sums under 5s.... ...	1	16	0
Mallon, John "Merccumbene"	1	0	0

BATHURST.

	£	s.	d.
Greville, W. C....	1	0	0
Mears, W....	1	1	0
Rutherford, J., J.P.... ...	1	1	0
Ramsay, G. F....	0	5	0
Parker, J.	0	5	0
Bonner, J....	0	5	0
Saunders, M.	0	5	0
Saville, G....	0	5	0
Henlen, F...	0	5	0
Bruce, R.	1	1	0

	£	s.	d.
Busby, J.	1	0	0
Oakes, R. and W.	0	10	0
Marsden, Mrs., senr. ...	0	10	0
Mason, W.	1	0	0
Vorbeck, L.	0	5	6
Morgan, W.	0	5	0
Simmons, C.	0	10	0
Pedrotta, B.	0	5	0
Jones, D.	0	10	0
Halliday, F. Mayor ...	0	5	0
Bassett, W. F., J.P. ...	1	0	0
Boylson, M., J.P.	0	10	0
Butterworth, H.	1	1	0
Jones, J. R.	0	5	0
Hales, T. B., J.P.	0	5	0
Marsh, J. M., P.M. ...	0	5	0
Tuckwell, S.	0	5	0
Fowler, W. J.	0	5	0
Fitzpatrick, J. F.	0	5	0
Paul, W. H.	0	5	0
Lydiard, C., J.P.	0	5	0
Morgan, Dr., J.P.	1	1	0
Pinnock, George	1	0	0
Price, H.	1	1	0
Jaye, J.	1	0	0
Richards, J. B., J.P. ...	1	1	0
Baldock, A.	0	5	0
White, J. C.	0	10	0
Kemmis, H., B.A. ...	0	10	0
Peate, L.	0	5	0
Cock, W.	1	0	0
Mutton, E. H.	0	5	0

	£	s.	d.
Webb, E., M.L.A.	1	1	0
Marsden, Right Rev. Bishop	1	0	0
Lamrock and Cornwell ...	0	5	0
Stanley, J.	0	5	0
Ranken, W. B., J.P. ...	0	10	0
Meagher, J.	0	10	0
Smith, Rev. Canon	0	10	0
Machattie, Dr.	0	10	6
Durack, F.	0	5	0
Durack, L.	0	5	0
Davidson, W. R., J.P. ...	1	1	0
Campbell, Archibald, J.P.	1	0	0
Well-wisher	0	5	0
Danse & McDougal... ...	0	5	0
Rae, A. B.	0	10	6
Alexander, J. L.	0	10	0
Thompson, W. G.	0	5	0
Palmer, J.	1	0	0
Bowler, Major, J.P. ...	1	0	0
Rotton, H., J.P.	1	1	0
McIntosh, J. N.	1	1	0
Sums under 5s.	0	10	0
Stewart, J. H., J.P., " The Mount "	1	0	0

BOWENFELLS.

	£	s.	d.
Corderoy, W., Bowenfells	1	0	0
Binning, Mrs. „	1	1	0
Hunt, Mrs. „	0	5	0
Cooke, C. „	0	5	0
Raymond, F. „	0	5	0
Gray, W. „	0	10	0
Horne, J. „	0	5	0
Lloyd, W. „	0	5	0
A Friend „	0	5	0
Brown, Andrew, J.P. „	2	0	0
Brown, Mrs. „	1	0	0
Brown, Miss „	1	0	0
Thompson, J. „	0	10	0

BRAIDWOOD.

	£	s.	d.
Byng, Rev. C. J.	0	5	0
Orridge, J. W. J.P.	0	10	0
Bassingthwaight, W. ...	0	5	0
A Friend	0	5	0
Gentle and Lewellyn, Drs.	1	1	0
Robson, Rev. W.	0	5	0
Phillpotts and Son	0	10	6
Sullivan, W.	0	5	0
Royds, E. M.	0	5	0
Gillham, H. K.	0	5	0
Clemenger, R. C.P.S. ...	0	5	0
Tweedie and Weston ...	1	1	0

	£	s.	d.
Hendricks, S. C.	0	5	0
McGrath, F.	0	5	0
Macleod, G. J.P.	0	10	6
Key, F.	0	5	0
Fairley, J....	1	0	0
Fox, Owen	0	5	0
Moseley, W.	0	5	0
Redman, A.	0	5	0
Merest, J. G.	0	5	0
Fell, W. C.	0	10	0
Scarvell, E. A.	1	1	0
Badgery, Mrs.	0	10	6
Rodd, G. P.	0	10	6
Wilson, H. P.	0	10	6
A Friend	0	5	0
McDouall, W.	0	5	0
Roberts, T. J.	1	1	0
Mason, Frank	1	1	0
O'Brien, J.	0	5	0
King, H.	0	5	0
Blatchford, J. H.	0	5	0
Basingthweight, George ...	0	5	0
Ryrie, Mrs., " Arnprior "	1	0	0
Cassels, Miss, ditto	0	10	0
Ryrie, J. C., ditto	0	5	0
Bruce, R.	0	5	0
Payne and Sandford... ...	1	0	0
Ella, Mrs.	0	5	0
Roberts, Mrs.	0	10	0
Stewart, Thos., J.P. "Highgate	0	10	0
Maddrell, R., J.P., "Bedervale "	1	1	0
Coghill, Mrs., per R. Maddrell	1	1	0
Maddrell, R. J. C., " Mona Cottage "	1	0	0
Fraser, John	0	10	0
Wallace, John, J.P., " Nithsdale "...	1	0	0
Griffin, Mrs.	0	5	0
Musgrave, J.	0	5	0
Geelen, R....	0	5	0
Edwards, Mrs.	0	5	0
Kertzmann and Maston ...	0	5	0
Clapham, R.	0	10	0
Fisher, B....	0	5	0
Darke, W....	0	10	0
Malone, James...	0	5	0
Tunks, A....	1	0	0
Sums under 5s....	1	7	6
Daly, Mrs., Jembaicumbene	0	5	0

	£	s.	d.
Percival, J., ditto	0	5	0
Rea, J. B., ditto	0	5	0
Mee War, ditto	0	5	0
Meyberry, J., Little River	0	5	0
McGrath, Mrs., ditto ...	0	10	0
Davies, W., ditto	0	10	0
Davies, W., collected by ditto	2	9	3
Garnett, Mrs., ditto... ...	0	10	0
Smith, J., ditto...	0	5	0
Cobb, H. A., Major's Creek	0	10	0
Hazlett, Mrs., ditto... ...	0	5	0
Slade, W. W., ditto... ...	0	10	6
Allan, J. S., ditto	0	10	0
T. H. B., ditto...	0	5	0
Forsyth, T., Bell's Creek...	0	10	0
Quong Tart, ditto	0	5	0

BUNGENDORE.

	£	s.	d.
Powell, N. S. J.P.	1	1	0
McJennett, J.	0	10	0
Smith, G....	0	10	0
Hayland, C.	0	5	0
McMahon, J.	0	5	0
Scott, C.	0	5	0
Burke, J. B.	0	10	0
McCluny, A.	0	5	0
Sums under 5s....	1	0	6
Hadden, J. Foxlow Station	0	10	0
Smith, J. ,,	0	5	0
Burns, M. ,,	0	5	0
Mabel, J. ,,	0	2	6
Osborne, A. ,,	0	5	0
Hopkins, J. ,,	0	5	0
Rutledge, Thomas, J.P. Carwoola	1	1	0
Treeby, C. Carwoola ...	0	2	6
Campbell, Mrs. George "Duntroon"...	2	2	0
Smith Rev. Pierce G. St. John's Parsonage ...	1	1	0
Gibbes, A. J.P., Yarra-lumla	2	0	0
Davis, W. J.P., Gunnada	1	1	0
Shanahan, T. The Briars	1	0	0
Allman, J. J. P.M.	1	0	0

BATEMAN'S BAY.

	£	s.	d.
Storey, W.	0	5	0
Guy, F.	0	10	0
Cowel, T. A.	0	5	0
Bourke, J. D.	0	5	0
McClaren, J.	0	5	0

	£	s.	d.
Haiser, G....	0	5	0
Sums under 5s....	0	17	0

DUBBO.

	£	s.	d.
Todhunter, M. J.P. " Wam-brina"	1	1	0
Tibbits, Dr. J.P.	0	10	6
Snow, J. T.	0	10	0
Poole, T.	0	5	0
Coen, M.	0	5	0
Page, H.	0	10	0
Samuels, A. C....	0	5	0
Tuck, W. H.	0	5	0
Guiness, Cecil " Murrum-bidgerie "	0	10	0
Baird, T. J.P., " Dundul-lima "	1	1	0
Thompson and Blacket ...	0	10	6
Links, G.	0	5	0
Readford, J. T.	0	5	0
Olver, W....	0	5	0
Peter, J.	0	5	0
Young, C....	0	5	0
Samuels, J. Senr.	0	5	0
Norton, J. O. P.M.... ...	0	5	0
Stevens and Co.	0	10	6
Liddell, A.	0	5	0
Browning, J. E.	0	5	0
Carr, J.	0	10	0
Fitzhardinge, C. H.... ...	0	10	0
Jones Brothers...	0	10	0
Moffatt, W.	0	10	0
Swift, H. L.	0	10	6
Muller, N.	0	10	6
Manning. T. and M. ...	0	10	0
Weavers, T. G.	0	5	0
Cloating, J. K....	0	5	0
Mitchell, R.	0	5	0
Taylor, G. H.	0	5	0
Goodisson, R. G.	0	10	0
Orbell, W. G.	1	0	0
Sums under 5s.	0	19	6
McKillop, D. J.P., Terra-bella	1	0	0
Gardiner, J. A. J.P., Go-bolion	1	0	0
Kerr, R. O. Lime Kilns ...	1	0	0
Shorter, W. T. A.	0	10	0
Cruickshank, A. J.P. ...	2	0	0

GERRINGONG.

	£	s.	d.
Wilson, Rev. K., Gerringong	0	10	0
Miller, William ,,	1	0	0

	£	s.	d.
Hindmarsh, K. Gerriugong	0	5	0
Hindmarsh, George ,,	0	10	0
Mc Nab, J. ,,	0	5	0
Lee, George ,,	0	5	0
Nelson, A. ,,	0	5	0
Davis, G. F. ,,	0	5	0
Hindmarsh, Thomas ,,	0	5	0
Hindmarsh, F. ,,	0	5	0
Sums under 5s....	0	9	6

GOULBURN.

	£	s.	d.
The Right Rev. the Lord Bishop of Goulburn ...	£1	1	0
Roberts, C. H....	0	10	0
Anderson, A.	1	1	0
Podmore, A., J.P.	0	5	0
Bull, J.	0	10	0
Bull, J., jun.	0	10	0
Woods, J....	0	5	0
Rev. Dean Sowerby ...	0	10	0
Cox, Mrs....	2	0	0
Barber, Miss	0	10	0
Waugh, Mrs.	0	10	0
Puddicombe, Rev. A. T....	0	10	0
DeLauret, A., J.P.	0	10	6
Norman, J.	0	10	0
Marsden, Thomas, J.P. ...	0	10	0
Morton, Dr. Selby M., J.P.	1	1	0
Twynam, E.	0	10	0
Banks, E....	1	1	0
Trenery, J. J....	0	10	0
Chisholm, William A., J.P.	1	0	0
Kinghorne, Alex., "Maxton"	0	10	0
Faithfull, W. P., J.P., Springfield	1	0	0
Emanuel, J. M.	0	10	0
Butler, E....	0	10	0
Dignam, P.	0	10	0
Payton, H.	0	10	0
Clarke, H. S.	0	10	0
Riley, W. R., Goulburn Herald	1	0	0
Antill, E. S., "Kenmore"	0	10	0
Newcombe, C. E., J.P. ...	1	0	0
Ross, Mrs...	0	10	0
Steer, Mrs.	0	5	0
Dickson, D., J.P.	0	10	0
Cohen, F. S.	1	1	0
Rankin, A. H., J.P., "Lockyersleigh"	1	1	0
Finlay, A. G., J.P.	1	1	0
Hayes, J. S., J.P.	1	0	0
Walker, C.	0	10	0

	£	s.	d.
Marks, Mrs.	0	10	0
Tecce, W., Senr.	0	10	0
Kirke, T.	0	5	0
Mackenzie, Rev. S. F. ...	0	10	6
Craig, Robert	0	10	0
Hunt, M.	0	5	0
Topham, G.	0	5	0
McAlister, R. T.	0	5	0
Walsh, John	0	5	0
Scowcroft, J.	0	5	0
Davies, Alexander & Co.	2	2	0
Employees—			
Brentnall, A. G.	0	10	6
Fleming, A. W.	0	5	0
Ralphill	0	1	0
Smith	0	2	6
Nosworthy	0	2	6
Rudd	0	2	6
A. C. H.	0	2	6
Hollis	0	2	6
Hicks, D. S.	0	10	0
Betts, A. M.	1	0	0
Jacobs, T. W.	0	5	0
Sprowle, A.	0	5	0
Hay, G. D.	0	10	0
Hayley, Dr. W. F. J.P. ...	0	10	6
Allen, J. T.	1	0	0
Gannou, J. T.	1	1	0
Rossi, Captain...	0	10	0
Buckley, Robert	0	10	0
Gibson, A. F. J.P.	1	1	0
Slocombe, John	0	5	0
Slocombe, G.	0	5	0
Slocombe, James	0	5	0
Stark, R. M.	0	5	0
Craig, Mrs. Salutation Inn	1	10	0
Conelly, W. J.P.	0	10	0
Thorn, Mrs.	0	10	0
Sums under 5s....	0	11	6
Deer, E. "Currawang " ...	1	0	0
Cooper Bros. "Willeroo "	2	0	0
Osborne, P. H. J.P. "Curraudooley "	2	2	0

GULGONG.

	£	s.	d.
Donaldson, L. S., J.P. ...	0	5	0
Per favour of Mrs. Newton—			
Rouse, Miss	1	1	0
Bellinfant, Dr.	2	2	0
Samper, S.	1	1	0
Rouse, G., J.P., "Guntawang "	1	0	0
Steuart	0	10	0
Clarke	0	10	0

	£	s.	d.
Bird, C....	0	10	0
Newton, Rev. W. S. ...	0	10	0
O'Neill, Brothers...	0	5	0
Robinson	0	5	0
Walker, W.	0	5	0
Osborne...	0	5	0
Mackulloch, A.	0	5	0
Green, Mrs.	0	5	0
Donaldson, L. S.. J.P....	0	5	0
Mills, Mrs.	0	5	0
Binder	0	5	0
Perkins	0	5	0
Jackson...	0	5	0
Johnson, A.	0	5	0
H. H.	0	2	6
Nailor, Mrs.	0	2	6
Plunkett, Mrs.	0	2	6
Children of Mrs. Plunkett	0	1	6
McMillan, Mrs.	0	2	6
Montgomery...	0	2	6
Lewis, W. T...	0	2	6
McGrath, E....	0	2	6
Cairnes, C. B.	0	.5	0
Sharman, G.	0	5	0
Pollock, Mrs. A.	0	5	0
Thomas, E.	0	5	0
Hill, J.	0	5	0
Davies, E....	0	5	0
Hunter, J.	0	5	0
Pericles, Dr.	0	10	6
Angove, R.	0	5	0
Young, C....	0	5	0
Driscoll, C.	0	5	0
Trevor, Rev. J.	0	10	0
Curtis, T. J.	0	5	0
Samper, S.	0	5	0
Walker, W. H....	0	5	0
Mc Kenzie, Mrs.	0	5	0
Langdon, K.	0	5	0
Self, W.	0	5	0
Sums under 5s. ..	0	11	0
Hawkins, W., Home rule	0	5	0
Sums under 5s. ,,	0	10	0
Piper, J., Lahys Creek ...	0	5	0
Davidson, Mrs., "Murrun-jundy"	0	10	0
Heane, James ,J.P., "Bar-bigal"	1	0	0

HILL END.

	£	s.	d.
Tress, Rev. T. B.	0	10	6
Chappell, T.	1	0	0
Shand, J.	0	5	0

	£	s.	d.
White and Howett	0	5	0
Manson, D.	0	7	6
Rawsthorne, R. J.	2	0	0
McKinnon, Rev. R.... ...	0	10	6
McLerie, A.	1	1	0
Haydon, T. J.	0	5	0
Dagner, Dr. C....	0	10	0
Rapp, J.	0	5	0
Steel, Alexander	0	5	0
Tallentire, J.	0	5	0
Brown, Mr. J. S.	0	5	0
Oxen, M.	0	10	0
Gondolf, P.	0	10	0
Stuart, H....	0	10	0
Wythes, T. Mayor	0	10	6
Ackerman, M....	0	10	0
Wythes, J.	0	5	0
Mayer, P....	0	5	0
Wilson, Rev. W.	0	10	0
Hill End Observer	0	10	0
Hill End Times, Advertis-ments free	0	8	0
Brand, R....	0	10	0
Sums under 5s.... ..	0	8	0
Suttor, T. C. junr., "Tri-amble"...	1	0	0
Campbell, J. "Millorang"	0	5	0

IRONBARKS.

	£	s.	d.
Landaner, S.	0	5	0
West, Mrs. J.	0	10	0
Hernfield, H.	0	5	0
Smith, J. W.	0	10	6
West, J.	0	10	0
Fleming, D.	0	5	0
Campbell, R.	0	5	0
Priest, J.	0	5	0
Buckley, Mrs. Stoney Ck.	0	5	0
Sums under 5s....	0	7	0

JAMBEROO.

	£	s.	d.
Calley, John	0	5	0
Stewart, W.	0	5	0
Braham, E.	0	5	0
A Friend	0	5	0
Davies, W.	0	5	0
Tate, E.	0	5	0
Dymock, D. L....	0	6	0
Tate, John	0	5	0
Dunlop, Thomas	0	10	0
Elliott, James	0	5	0
Sums under 5s.	0	6	6

KIAMA.

	£	s.	d.
Zillman, Rev. J. H. L. ...	0	5	0
Chapman, T., J.P.	1	0	0
Kendall, Thomas, J.P. ...	0	10	0
Keogan, Rev. Father ...	0	5	0
Stewart, J. G.	0	5	0
Brown, Rev. J. W.	0	10	0
Hayes, W., J.P.	0	5	0
Wood, George, Spring Hill	0	5	0
Craig, N.	0	5	0
Marks, John, J.P.	1	1	0
A Friend	0	5	0
Gray, W.	0	5	0
Hindmarsh, N.	0	5	0
E. W.	0	5	0
Black, John, J.P.	0	10	6
Grey, George	0	10	6
A. M.	0	5	0
Fuller, T. J.	0	10	0
Redford, J.	0	5	0
Hincks, J.	0	5	0
McIntyre, W.	0	10	0
King, W. E.	1	1	0
A Friend	0	5	0
Weston, J.	0	5	0
Haydon, A.	0	5	0
Reid, S.	0	5	0
Colley, James, J.P.	0	5	0
Pike, Joseph, Mayor ...	1	0	0
Major, S.	0	5	0
Newburn, A. W.	0	5	0
Morrison, A.	0	5	0
Adams, Mrs.	0	10	6
Charles, Captain, J.P. ...	0	10	0
Sums under 5s.	0	17	0

KELSO.

	£	s.	d.
Denny, Thomas	1	1	0
Kite, Thomas, senr.	1	0	0
Cass, Rev. A.	0	5	0
Vines, P.	0	10	0
Matthews, G.	0	10	0
Bruce, H.	0	5	0
Parker, J.	0	5	0
Davey, J.	0	5	0
Thompson, Mrs.	0	10	6
Thompson, G. A.	0	10	6
Lee, W.	0	10	0
Lee, Mrs. George	1	0	0
Lee, George	0	10	6
Nash, C. Macquarie Plains	1	0	0
Webb, Mrs., ,,	0	5	0
West, J., sen., J.P. ,,	1	1	0

	£	s.	d.
Gatty, M., Poel	0	10	0
Suttor, T. C., ,, ...	1	0	0
Suttor, W. H., J.P., "Bruce-			
dale"	2	2	0
Suttor, J. B., J.P. "Wyag-			
don"	1	0	0
Prince, J., Wattle Flat ...	0	5	0
Ray, H. J. ,, ,, ...	0	5	0
Musgrave, T. ,, ,, ...	0	5	0
Sums under 5s. ,, ...	0	6	0

MILTON.

	£	s.	d.
Ewin, W., J.P. "Wood-			
stock"	1	1	0
McArthur, A.	0	5	0
Miller, J., J.P.	0	10	0
Kendall, W.	0	10	0
Hobbs, F.	0	5	0
Fitch, C.	0	5	0
Wheatley, W. A.	0	10	0
Seacombe, R.	0	10	6
Rodenham, W. W.	1	1	0
Hall, F.	1	1	0
Mitchell, T.	0	5	0
McMahan, F., J.P.	1	0	0
Claydon, H.	0	10	0
Vick, J. W.	0	5	0
Evans, J.	0	10	0
Allen, J. "Danesbank" ...	0	10	6
Hobbs, Thomas "Apenel"	0	10	6
Warden, D., J.P.	1	1	0
Cooper, M. A.	0	5	0
Falk, J.	0	5	0
Simmons, George	0	10	6
McLean, A., J.P.	0	10	0
McLean, Mrs., Senr. ...	0	10	0
Sheaffe, Capt., J.P.	0	5	0
Kendall, John, J.P. "Ken-			
dalldale...	0	10	0
Parnell, John, Tomerang	0	10	0
Craig, M. ... ... ,, ...	0	5	0
Sums under 5s.	0	9	6
Brown, John M. "Parma"	1	0	0

MOLONG.

	£	s.	d.
Finch, T.	0	5	0
Boyce, Rev. F. B.	0	5	0
Haslam, J.	0	10	0
Peckham, H.	0	10	0
Peckham, C. H.	0	5	0
Rubie, J.	0	5	0
Farmer, W. junr.	0	10	0
Smith, L. N. "Boree" ...	0	10	0

	£	s.	d.
Bell, W.	0	5	0
Rollo, W. J.	0	10	0
Kinnear, Dr.	0	5	0
Parslow, J.	0	5	0
Blakefield, C.	1	0	0
Parker, A....	0	5	0
Wynne, J...	0	5	0
Phillips, Mrs. H.	0	10	6
Bowler, J....	0	5	0
Kite, T., junr., "Kangaroo-bic"	10	10	0
Ashcroft, J., "Cannonbar"	1	0	0
Sums under 5s....	0	13	6

MUDGEE.

	£	s.	d.
Branscombe, W.	0	5	0
Schlachter, F.	0	10	0
Kellett, W.	0	5	0
Tuckerman, S. E.	0	5	0
White, R. H. D., J.P. ...	1	1	0
Potter, S.	1	0	0
Lester, W. R.	0	10	0
Warburton, George, P.M.	0	5	0
Lane, James	0	5	0
Smith, J.	0	5	0
Nicholson, M. L.	0	5	0
Daly, E.	0	5	0
Brown, J....	0	5	0
Cadell, W. B.	1	0	0
McEwen, Rev. Alexander	1	1	0
Spickett, J. D. and Co. ...	1	1	0
Little, D.	0	5	0
Sheppard, M. J.	0	10	0
Woods, J. T.	0	10	6
Woods, W. F....	0	10	6
Dickson, Mrs. Senr. ...	1	1	0
Cox, Hon. G. H., M.L.C. "Burrundulla"	2	2	0
Cox, V., J.P.	0	10	0
Crossing, H.	0	10	0
Crossing, J.	0	10	0
Cutting, Dr.	1	0	0
Arnold Brothers	0	5	0
Bishop, W.	0	5	0
Cox, A. H., J.P.	2	0	0
Cox, C. C.. J.P...	1	0	0
Sherry and Neelthorpe ...	0	10	0
Rankin, A. C.	0	5	0
Hughson, R. R...	0	10	0
Laurence, F.	0	5	0
Lawson, C. W., J.P., "Putta Bucca"	1	0	0
Sums under 5s....	0	2	6

MORUYA.

	£	s.	d.
Love, Rev. J. G.	0	10	0
Gannon, T. T. J.P.	0	5	0
Emmott, A.	0	10	0
McKeon, J. J.P.	0	5	0
Lodge, T. C.	0	5	0
Halloran, E. R...	0	5	0
Caswell, W. S. P.M. ...	0	10	0
Clements, W. J.	0	5	0
Lindo, A. P.	0	5	0
Alerdyce, Rev. A.	0	5	0
Boot, E.	0	5	0
Humphries, J.P., School Master, Church of England School	0	10	0
Children of ditto ditto ...	0	12	0
Coxon, M. A.	0	5	0
Coman, J....	0	5	0
Hanagan, W. T., J.P. ...	0	5	0
Sums under 5s....	1	6	6

MOUNT VICTORIA.

	£	s.	d.
Perry, John	0	10	0
Lewington, W., Little Hartley...	1	1	0
Fryer, R. F., Kerosene Works	0	5	0
Neale, T. H., P.M., Hartley	0	5	0
Sums under 5s. ,,	1	1	0

NELLIGAN.

	£	s.	d.
Manning, Mrs. C. M. ...	0	7	0
Olley, J.	0	5	0
Gibson, A. T.	0	10	6
Hunter, G.	0	5	0
Webber, George, J.P. ...	0	10	0
Sums under 5s....	0	3	6
Evans, E., "Murramaraug"	0	5	0

ORANGE.

	£	s.	d.
Shallanbertz, C.	1	0	0
Robinson & Kinealy, Messrs.	0	10	0
Employees of Messrs. R. & K.	0	13	6
Evans, W. T., C.P.S. ...	1	0	0
Russell, C. W....	1	1	0
Tipper, A....	0	5	0
Poulton, J. A. H.	0	10	6
Kerrman, M. "Coonamble"	1	0	0
Couleon, A.	0	10	0
Warren, Dr. J.P.	1	1	0
Higgins, Mrs.	0	5	0
Goddard, F.	0	5	0

	£	s.	d.
McLachlan, J. C.	0	10	0
Windred, J.	0	6	6
Frost, R.	1	0	0
Dale, James, J.P.	1	0	0
Whitney, W. F.	1	0	0
Conley, J.	0	10	0
Wallace, W.	0	10	0
Webb, T. G., J. P. Gyong	1	0	0
Kerr, Andrew, J. P. ...	1	0	0
Herrick, J.	0	5	0
Clifton, Rev. J. ...	0	10	0
Skipper, J. B.	0	5	0
Parker, J.	0	10	6
Warren, W.	0	10	6
Downs, R.	0	5	0
Grassick, J.	0	10	0
Tennant, Dr.	1	1	0
Tom, W., J.P.	0	5	0
Hale, W. M.	0	5	0
Moulder, W.	1	1	0
Nathan, E.	0	6	0
Torpy, J.	0	10	0
Whiteford, R. J.	0	5	0
Lane, C. W.	0	5	0
Gilleland, J.	0	5	0
Bowen, M. B.	1	0	0
Sums under 5s....	0	7	0
Hawke, G. junr., Lucknow	0	10	0
Newman, H. W. ,,	0	10	0
Blunt, C. ,,	0	10	0
Kinghorn, W. ,,	0	5	0
Sums under 5s. ,,	0	4	6
Hawke, G. J.P. Pondarves			
Byng	1	1	0
Young, L. C., Guyong ...	0	5	0
Tanner, Mrs. ,,	0	10	0

Employees of Messrs. Dalton Brothers Orange.

	£	s.	d.
Treuens, Miss	0	2	6
Emmes, J.	0	5	0
O'Connor, J. F.	0	2	6
Daly, W.	0	2	6
West, W.	0	2	6
Bernasconi, W.	0	5	0
Fullarton, A.	0	2	6

QUEANBEYAN.

Collected by Mr. W. G. O'Neill.

	£	s.	d.
Soares, Rev. A. D.	£1	1	0
Smith, Rev. P. G., M.A...	1	1	0
Russell, Colonel, P.M. ...	1	1	0
Rutledge, Mr. Thomas ...	1	1	0

	£	s.	d.
Gale, Mr. John	1	1	0
DeSalis, Mr. L. W., M.P.	1	0	0
Gibbes, Mr. A., J.P. ...	1	0	0
Cunningham, Mr. A., J.P.	1	0	0
Ryrie, Mr. A., J.P.	1	0	0
Connolly, Mrs. R.	1	0	0
Allan, Master G. R... ...	1	0	0
Allan, Master J. McF. ...	1	0	0
Harcourt, Mr. George ...	1	0	0
Jordan, Mr. Thomas ...	1	0	0
McKeahnie, Mr. A. A. J.P.	0	10	6
Davis, Mr. Wm., J.P. ...	0	10	6
O'Neill, Mr. W. G.... ...	0	10	6
McCarthy, Mr. W. R., J.P.	0	10	6
Barnett, Mr. William ...	0	10	6
Mehegan, Mr. R.	0	10	6
Morton, Dr. A., M.D., J.P.	0	10	6
Newton, Dr. J. L., M.D...	0	10	6
Cartwright, Mr. J.	0	10	6
McMichael, Rev. T. R. ...	0	10	0
McKellar, Mr. R. W. ...	0	10	0
M'Keahnie, Mr. C.	0	10	0
O'Rourke, Mr. J.	0	10	0
Nugent, Mr. J. W.... ...	0	10	0
Cane, Mr. Henry	0	10	0
Cameron, Mr. K.	0	10	0
Shanahan, Mr. T. (the Briers)	0	10	0
Happy Home Lodge Odd-fellows	0	10	0
McNamara, Mr. J.	0	10	0
Naylor, Mr. P....	0	10	0
Willans, Mr. O.	0	10	0
Heslop, Mr. F....	0	10	0
Southwell, Mr. T.	0	5	0
Wright, Mr. J. J., J.P. ...	0	5	0
Duff, Mr. M.	0	5	0
Ward, Mr. E. M.	0	5	0
Gabriel, Mr. A. W.... ...	0	5	0
McDonald, Mr. J.	0	5	0
Geary, Mr. James	0	5	0
Wittington, Mr. E	0	5	0
Woodward, Mr. J. J. ...	0	5	0
Edmunds, Mr. F. J.... ...	0	5	0
Spratt, Mr. J. B.	0	5	0
Hollett, Mr. William ...	0	5	0
Parker, Mr. D....	0	5	0
Byrne, Mr. J. J.	0	5	0
Land, Mr. E.	0	5	0
Wilson, Mr. T....	0	5	0
Holland, Mr. W. J... ...	0	5	0
Buttle, Mr. T.	0	5	0
Brown, Mr. J....	0	5	0

	£	s.	d.
Wiseman, W. J.	0	5	0
Commens, Messrs.	0	5	0
Woodward, F.	0	7	6
Parsons, R.	0	5	0
Chambers, S.	0	5	0
Robertson, W. G.	0	10	0
Hewlett, George	0	10	0
Hewlett, W.	0	10	0
Bow, W. R.	0	5	0
Waldron, A.	0	5	0
Scott, P.	0	5	0
Beatson, A.	0	5	0
Cole, F. R.	0	10	0
Davies, Mrs.	0	10	0
Sums under 5s.	1	6	6
Fry, H., Woonona	0	5	0
Levey, B. F. „	0	10	0
Turnbull, R., Bulli	0	5	0
Spier, C. H. „	0	5	0
Sums under 5s. „	0	2	6
Poulton, J., Appin	0	5	0
Clayton, Mrs. F. M.			
"Rockwood" „	0	10	0
Vickery, Mrs. M. „ „	0	5	0
Sums under 5s. „	0	2	6
Reddall, Misses, "Glen			
Alpiu"	1	0	0
Fowler, G. R., Campbell-			
town	0	10	0
Fowler, D. „	0	10	0
Roach, Rev. Father „	1	0	0

PARRAMATTA.

	£	s.	d.
Manton, Mrs.	0	5	0
Houison, J.	2	2	0
Fullagar, W., J.P.	0	10	0
Günther, Rev. W. J. ...	0	10	6
Burge, W. C.	0	5	0
Burge, S., Mayor	0	10	0
Golledge, J. J.P.	1	0	0
Ritchie, R. A.	0	10	0
Waugh, Dr.	0	10	0
Purchase, Mrs....	0	5	0
Oakes, Mrs., senr.	0	5	0
Fuller, C. E.	0	5	0
Neale, J., J.P.	1	10	0
Rowling, E. L. J.P... ...	0	10	0
Brown, Dr. W...	1	0	0
Bowden, J. E., J.P.... ...	0	10	0
Stewart, N., J.P.	1	0	0
Pye, James, Alderman ...	1	0	0
Tamsett, J	0	5	0

	£	s.	d.
Clift, J.	0	5	0
Pearce, M...	0	10	0
Pearce J.	0	5	0
Rouse, Mrs.	2	0	0
Hellyer, T. H.	0	10	0
Pass, J. W.	0	10	0
Whitworth, J.	0	10	0
Payten, N...	0	10	0
Bettington, Mrs.	2	0	0
Sharp, J. P.	0	5	0
Spurway, W.	0	5	0
Darvall, Mrs.	2	2	0
Galloway, James, Alderman	1	0	0
Sums under 5s...	1	3	6
	£24	8	0

GLADESVILLE.

	£	s.	d.
Manning, Dr., Gladesville	£1	1	0
Betts, E. M., ditto	0	5	0
Bland, Mrs., ditto	0	5	0
McGeorge, ditto	0	5	0
Watson, G. C., Ryde ...	0	5	0
Pope, G. N., C.P.S., ditto	0	5	0
A Friend, ditto	0	5	0
Forster, Mrs.	1	0	0
A Friend, ditto	0	10	0
	4	1	0
Sums under 5s.	0	6	0
	£4	7	0

WINDSOR.

	£	s.	d.
Smith, W. K., J.P., Clydes-			
dale	1	1	0
A Friend	1	0	0
Lamrock, W. J.P.	0	10	0
Neilson, J. T.	0	10	0
Dickson, G.	0	5	0
Robinson and Greenwell...	0	10	6
Beard, W., junr.	0	10	0
Onus, J. E.	0	10	0
Ridge, R., J.P....	1	0	0
Bowman, F. W.	0	10	0
Tebbutt, John	1	0	0
Egerton, Captain S... ...	0	5	0
Busby, J. S.	0	5	0
Nugent, N.	0	10	0
Liddell, James	0	5	0
Turner, Mrs.	0	10	0
Raper, E., J.P...	0	5	0

	£	s.	d.		£	s.	d.
Gow, John	0	10	0	Arndell, T.	0	7	6
Henson, G. R.	0	5	0	Thomas, W. R., C.P.S. ...	0	5	0
Hannabus, John	0	5	0	Harris, J.	0	5	0
Hobbs, Joseph, Pitt Town	0	5	0	Cullen, Rev. J. F.	0	5	0
Wood, Rev. W., ditto ...	1	0	0	Fitzgerald, Rev. P.	0	5	0
Chaseling, Thomas, ditto...	0	5	0	Dean, W.	0	5	0
Moore, Rev. D., ditto ...	0	10	0	Selkirk, Dr. J.	1	1	0
Hall, James, ditto	0	10	0	May, C. W.	0	5	0
Hart, Alfred A., ditto ...	0	5	0	Bowlin, J.	0	10	0
Dunstan, James, ditto ...	0	5	0	Holmes, J.	0	5	0
Ascough, James, J.P. ...	0	5	0	Pye, D.	0	5	0
Garnsey, Rev. C. F., 1872-				Sums under 5s...	2	14	0
73-74	3	0	0				
					£23	4	0

SCHOOL FEES, &c.

	£	s.	d.		£	s.	d.
Arrel, Mrs.	2	10	0	Kluga, Mrs., (Clothing) ...	1	9	0
Allison, Mrs., (Music) ...	4	0	0	Ditto, (Fee)	2	10	0
Ditto, (Fee)	11	0	0	Moore, Mr. S., (Clothing)	1	10	0
Byrnes, George	6	7	6	Ditto, (Fee)	25	0	0
Britcheno, Mr.	4	0	0	Morgan, Mrs.	1	0	0
Bridgement, Mr.	6	5	0				
Churchill, H., (Clothing)	2	10	4	Pollack, James...	3	0	0
Ditto, (Fee)	5	0	0	Queensland Government...	66	10	0
Driscoll, J.	1	6	6	Ryan, Mrs.	3	0	0
Durham, F.	2	15	3	Ruwald, Capt., (Clothing)	0	13	0
Darcy, Mr.	6	0	0	Ditto, (Fee)	25	0	0
Ellis, Mr.	1	14	4	Read, Mrs.	6	6	0
Everingham, Mr.	3	0	0	Rodgers, Mr.	1	0	0
Farr, J. J.	15	0	0				
Fitzpatrick, Mr.	2	10	0	Smart, Mr.	0	11	6
Goldsworthy, Mrs.	1	11	6	Smith, Mr. C. H.	10	0	0
Ditto, (Fee)...	5	10	0	Sparke, Mrs.	0	14	10
Golding, Charles	3	15	0	Smails, Mrs.	1	2	6
Hurst, Rev. G.	45	0	0	Selby, Mr., (Clothing) ...	3	6	0
Howe, Mr., (Clothing) ...	0	5	4	Tasmanian Government ...	28	0	0
Ditto, (Fee)	2	15	0				
Hicks, Mr.	0	10	6	White, Mrs., (Fee)	3	15	0
Jones, Mrs., (Clothing) ...	0	5	4	Ditto, (Clothing)	0	2	6
Ditto, (Fee)	8	0	0	Wehrman, —	1	12	4
Jamison, Mrs.	2	0	0	Worsley, Mr. S.	2	12	0
				Wilbow, Mrs.	3	2	6

MISCELLANEOUS DONATIONS.

Received during the year ending September 30th, from the following, and thankfully acknowledged :—

Howe, Mr., a Dove Cote, also *Illustrated London News*, copies of from Mr. Banks.

Patterson, Mr., Harmonieon for Blind Children.

Newton, Mrs., Packages of Lollies.

Alexander, Mrs. M., Buns, Cake, &c.

Hay, Mrs., Sweets, Buns, &c. at different times.

Moore, Mr. S., Several Cases of Oranges and other fruit, also Quantity Potatoes, Vegetables, &c.

Danger, Mr. F. C., Large quantity of Fruit, Cake, Sweets for Christmas treat.

Dickson, Mrs., Articles, requisite for Christmas Pudding, also fruit at other times

Wigzell, Mr., Buns. He kindly cuts Children's hair monthly.

Metcalfe, Mrs., Cases of fruit at various times, also numbers of *Illustrated London News*.

Slocombe, Mr., Honey and Fruit.

Jones, Mr. H., Case of Peaches.

Messrs. Meyerfeld & Co., 1 Bag Rice, ¼ Chest Tea, and 1 Bag Sago.

Holt, Miss, Buns for Good Friday.

Dickson, Mrs., ditto ditto.

Craig, Mrs., Jam.

Stuart, Mrs. A., Case of Oranges.

Palser, Mrs. ditto ditto.

Elouis, Mr., Cases of Oranges and Apples, also Cake &c. for Treat for Children.

Henry, Mr., Dentistry for Children Gratis.

Gratuitous Copies of *Illustrated Sydney News*, also *Sydney Mail*, and *Australian Churchman*, from the proprietors.

Goodlett, Mrs.,
Baillie, Mrs., } Special Prizes for proficiency in Needle Work and School
Sampson, Mrs., } Work.
Campbell, Miss,

W. H. Paling, Repairs to Piano Forte, gratuitous.

Lewis Moss, Tuning ditto, ditto.

Work done by the Girls in the Institution during the year ending 30th September, 1874 :—

17 Dresses	9 Pairs of Trousers
4 Petticoats	20 Sheets
12 Pairs of Drawers	41 Pillow Cases
14 Chemises	4 Pairs of Stays
3 Night Dresses	3 Vests
13 Pinafores	8 Night Shirts
12 Aprons	2 Jackets
3 Coats	20 Towels, &c.

PRIZE FUND.

Alexander, M. Esq., J.P.	...	...	...	...	£1	0	0				
Linsley, Mr. Alderman	...	...	...	...	1	0	0				
Rae, Mr. William	...	...	...	...	...	1	0	0			
Hills, Mr. R.	...	...	...	...	...	1	0	0			
								£4	0	0
Expended in Prizes for the Annual Examination, 1872 ...						...		1	10	2
Balance in hand				...	...	...		2	9	10
Hon. Secretary's donation			...	...	...		0	5	2
								2	15	0
Expended for Prizes at Annual Examination, Dec. 1873...						...		2	15	0

N.B.—The Prize Fund is exhausted.

NEW SOUTH WALES

INSTITUTION for the DEAF and DUMB, and the BLIND.

INFORMATION RELATING TO APPLICATIONS FOR THE ADMISSION OF PUPILS TO THE INSTITUTION, &c., &c.

1. Applications must be in writing addressed to the Secretary, and should contain as full information as possible, the necessary forms can be obtained of the Hon. Secretary.

2. Pupils are admissible from any part of the colony of New South Wales, and under certain conditions, from Queensland, Tasmania, and New Zealand.

3. No child deficient in intellect can be considered a fit subject for admission.

4. Children from five to twelve years of age are eligible for admission, but in no case shall the age be above 15 years.

5. No order will be given by the Committee for a child's admission until the medical certificate has been obtained.

6. Children on entering the Institution are required to have two complete suits of clothing, for school or week-day wear, to be of dark colour, and a better suit for Sunday, and must be provided with clothing (see list) by their parents or friends during their residence, each child must be provided with a Box or Trunk in which to keep clean clothing for use.

7. Any amounts remitted to the Secretary for the purchase of clothing will be expended under the direction of the Committee of Management.

8. The fees payable in ordinary cases for the board, education, &c., of children in the Institution are:—Under seven years of age, £20 per annum; over seven years of age, £25 per annum; in special cases a lower scale of fees is adopted.

9. In the case of pauper children, a certificate of inability to pay any fee must be obtained from known individuals.

10. The fees are payable in advance, and date from the time of admission.

11. Children cannot be permitted to leave the Institution unless with the direct sanction and authority of the Committee.

12. In addition to the usual educational course the girls are taught household duties, and the boys out-door and other work.

13. It is essential that pupils should return to the Institution on the day fixed to commence duties after each vacation, and with their clothing clean and in proper order.

14. The average term of residence in the Institution is for Deaf and Dumb pupils 6 to 8 years, and for Blind pupils 3 to 5 years.

ELLIS ROBINSON,
Hon. Secretary.

NEW SOUTH WALES

Institution for the Deaf and Dumb and the Blind,

NEWTOWN ROAD.

The following quantity of Clothing is required for each child, to be supplied on its entering the Institution, which it is anticipated will last for twelve months :—

For Boys.	*For Girls.*
2 Suits for week-day wear	3 Dresses for week-day wear
1 Suit for Sunday ditto	1 Dress for Sunday ditto
4 Shirts, day—white or crimean	2 Petticoats, general use
2 Night ditto	1 Petticoat, Sunday ditto
6 Pairs Socks	6 Pairs Stockings or Socks
2 Caps or Felt Hats	2 Hats
6 Collars	6 Plain Linen Collars or Frills
6 Handkerchiefs	6 Handkerchiefs
2 Pairs Cotton Braces	1 Warm Jacket
2 Neckties	6 Pairs Drawers
1 Hair and 1 Tooth Brush	2 Pairs Stays or Bodies
1 Rack and 1 Fine Tooth Comb.	3 Chemises
For Small Boys.	6 Pinafores or Aprons
3 Holland Pinafores may be supplied.	1 Rack and 1 Fine Tooth Comb
	1 Hair and 1 Tooth Brush.

Each child to be provided with a Box or Trunk in which to keep Clothing when clean for use. The Clothing in all cases must be Dark Coloured. The Girls' dresses may be Print for Summer wear, and Alpaca, Wincey, or similar material for Winter wear.

Boys' suits should be of Dark Coloured washing Tweed or other similar material. (Drill suits are not to be worn.)

ELLIS ROBINSON,

March 31st, 1873.   *Honorary Secretary.*

SPECIAL INFORMATION.

"The object of this Institution is the educating, and maintenance whilst so doing, of Deaf and Dumb and Blind children, from the age of five years; to enable them to earn their own living, make them useful members of society, and prevent them becoming, as they would in most cases, a burden upon public charity in after years."

The Institution is open to Subscribers and other Visitors daily—Saturdays, Sundays, and holidays excepted,—from 2 to 4 p.m.

The Parents and Friends of children are admitted once a fortnight, on Thursdays, between the hours of 12 noon and 3 p.m.

The Children are permitted to visit their Friends once a month, on special application being made to the Committee.

Forms and all particulars for the admission of pupils into the Institution can be obtained of the Honorary Secretary.

Subscriptions and Donations will be thankfully received and acknowledged by the Treasurer, the Secretary, or at the Institution.

The Meetings of Committee are held on the Second Monday in each month, at 4 o'clock p.m. The Ladies Visiting Committee meet at the Institution, on the last Friday in the month, at 3 o'clock in the Winter and half-past 3 o'clock in the Summer months.

All communications to be addressed to Mr. Ellis Robinson, Honorary Secretary, at the Institution, or 486, George street, Sydney.

Money orders should be made payable to the Secretary or Treasurer at the Head Office, Post Office, St. Martin's, Sydney.

Donations of Meat, Vegetables, Fruit (Fresh and Preserved,) are thankfully received and acknowledged; also Clothing and Materials for the same will be thankfully accepted.

RULES AND REGULATIONS

OF THE

NEW SOUTH WALES

Institution for the Deaf & Dumb, & the Blind.

~~~~~~~~~~~~~~~~~~

NAME AND OBJECT.

1. This Institution shall be called the New South Wales Institution for the Deaf and Dumb, and the Blind, having for its object the education of Deaf and Dumb, and Blind Children, and shall be under the management of a Committee to be constituted in manner hereinafter mentioned.

AGE OF CHILDREN.

2. No Child shall be admitted of an age younger than five years, nor older than twelve years, unless under special circumstances, to be decided by the Committee ; but in no case shall the age at admission exceed fifteen years.

MEMBERS.

3. Every Subscriber of one pound per annum, shall be a Member of the Institution, and every Donor of twenty pounds in one payment, shall be a Life Member.

OFFICERS AND BOARD OF MANAGEMENT.

4. i. The Officers of the Institution, shall consist of one President, one or more Vice-Presidents, a Treasurer, and a Secretary, all of whom shall be elected at the Annual General Meeting, and shall, *ex officio*, be Members of the Board of Management.

ii. In addition to the 20 Members of Committee, there shall be appointed " Life Directors " entitled to hold office under the following circumstances, and with the privilege of attending and voting at all Meetings of Committee.

iii. As the Founders of the Institution, and who have been continuous Members of Committee since the foundation.

iv. For 5 years continuous services as an Honorary Treasurer or Honorary Secretary of the Institution.

v. for 10 years continuous services as a Member of Committee provided they have attended no less than 4 Meetings of Committee each year.

vi. As Contributor of a Donation in one payment of £50.

vii. By Resolution of Committee for special services rendered to the Institution.

The names of all such Life Directors to be published each year in the Annual Report, also included in a Life Directors' List on a Tablet in the Hall of the Institution.

5. i. The Committee or Board of Management shall consist of not less than Eight nor more than Twenty Members to be elected at the Annual General Meeting—The Names of Members so to be elected shall be submitted for the approval of the Committee at its meeting immediately previous to the Annual Meeting—Notice being given at a former meeting of any new member intended to be proposed.

ii. Any vacancy occuring during the year to be filled up by the Committee at the monthly meeting, notice being given at the previous meeting of the name of the Member intended to be proposed to fill such vacancy.

iii. That the Five members who have attended the least number of Committee Meetings during the year shall retire, but be eligible for re-election.

iv. That no person shall be qualified to be nominated as a Member of Committee, whose subscription has not been paid for the past Financial year.

COMMITTEE MEETINGS.

6. The Committee shall meet monthly, (or oftener if necessary) for the transaction of business. Three members to form a quorum.

POWER OF COMMITTEE.

7. The Committee shall have the power of appointing and dismissing the Master, Matron, Assistants, or servants ; shall receive applications for the admission of children, and shall decide upon them.

QUESTIONS.

8. All questions before the Committee shall be decided by a majority of votes, the chairman, in case of need, having a casting vote.

MEDICAL OFFICER.

9. There shall be at least one Honorary Medical Officer, who shall be elected at the Annual General Meeting, and who shall *ex officio*, be a member of the Committee. His duties will be to attend at the Institution, and give the necessary advice when any of the children are sick.

LADIES' VISITING COMMITTEE.

10. A Ladies' Visiting Committee, consisting of not more than twenty, shall be elected by the Committee of Management, to superintend the domestic arrangements of the Institution, to meet monthly or oftener, and report in writing to the Committee, any suggestion for the benefit of the Institution.

CANDIDATES FOR ADMISSION.

11. All candidates for admission shall be recommended (in the form provided) by two members of the Institution and by a Clergyman or Magistrate of the District in which the candidates reside, who shall be required to fill up certain forms for the information of the Committee of Management; and no child shall be admitted who shall not previously have received the requisite certificate from the Honorary Medical Officer of the Institution.

FEES.

12. Children whose parents are, in the opinion of the Committee unable to pay, shall be received, boarded, and educated gratuitously. Children

whose parents are able to pay, shall be charged as follows, viz. :— Under 7 years of age, £20 per annum. Over 7 years, £25 per annum; or such other payments as the Committee may decide. But in every case the parents must provide clothing for their children.

VISITORS.

13. Parents or Friends of children, shall be allowed to visit them once a fortnight, on Thursdays, between the hours of 12 noon and 3 p.m., in the presence of the Master or Matron.—Subscribers and other Visitors shall be admitted on any day, Saturdays, Sundays, and holidays excepted, between the hours of 2 and 4 p.m.

VACATIONS.

14. The Vacations shall be for five weeks at Christmas, and for one week at Mid-winter.

ANNUAL MEETING.

15. The Annual General Meeting shall be held each year, in the month of October, or as soon after as the Committee may deem desirable, at which meeting the Report of the Committee and the audited Accounts of the Treasurer for the past year shall be presented, and such other business transacted as may be brought before the Meeting by the Committee of Management.

AUDITORS.

16. Two Auditors shall be appointed annually by the Committee to audit the Treasurer's Accounts previous to the Annual Meeting.

THE TREASURER.

His Duties shall be—

1. To pay all monies received by him on behalf of the Institution into the Commercial or other Bank, as directed by the Committee, in the name of the New South Wales Institution for the Deaf and Dumb, and the Blind.

2. To furnish at each monthly Meeting of the Committee an account of the receipts and payments since the previous meeting, showing the then state of the funds of the Institution, and producing the Bank Book in verification of the same.

3. To pay all accounts when passed by the Committee, and certified by the Chairman, by cheques to be signed by the Treasurer and the Secretary.

4. To prepare Statement of the year's accounts, and submit the same, with the requisite Vouchers, to the Auditors, previous to the Annual General Meeting.

THE SECRETARY.

His Duties shall be—

1. To attend the meetings of the Committee, to keep the minutes of the proceedings, and conduct the correspondence of the Institution.

2. To summon all meetings, and to prepare the business to be brought before the Committee.

3. To have the custody of all documents, books and property of the Institution.

4. To order all necessary Stores, Furniture and supplies for the Institution according to the direction of the Committee, and to carry out the instructions of the Committee, and have the general superintendence of the Institution.

RULES.

No alteration of, or addition to, the preceding rules shall be made without the sanction of a majority of the Committee.

RULES FOR THE INTERNAL GOVERNMENT OF THE INSTITUTION.

Duties of Officers.

THE MASTER.

I.—Shall be appointed by, and responsible to the Committee—and his duties are,—That he shall have the Supervision of the whole Establishment, together with any other duties that the Committee of Management may from time to time direct.

II.—He will be present in School at the hours appointed, and be responsible for the full and effective discharge of all duties connected with the school-room; and will be courteous in explaining the system of instruction to all visitors.

III.—He will accompany the Protestant boys each Sunday to church (weather permitting) and will conduct Sunday School on Sunday afternoons.

IV.—He will be responsible that good order and discipline are maintained in the Institution.

V.—He will have charge of the boys during their time of recreation in the play-ground, and will check any irregularity, or improper conduct, and encourage cheerful and innocent amusement, and will accompany the boys for a walk (weather permitting) once each week.

VI.—He will be held responsible for, and will have the charge of the keys of the outer doors and gates after the same have been locked by him at night.

VII.—The Gas-burners throughout the Building, shall be managed and regulated by the Master, who shall turn off the gas each night.

VIII.—He will supervise the boys in carrying out all such Industrial pursuits as may be sanctioned or directed to be made by the Committee.

IX.—He will keep a House Journal, to be laid before the Committee at their monthly Meetings, detailing all daily occurrences, and will specially note the weekly progress of the children at school.

X.—In all matters not specified in these Rules, he shall act under the direction of the Committee.

THE MATRON.

I.—The Matron shall be appointed by the Committee, and to her shall be entrusted the entire direction of the household, to the business of which she shall direct her whole time and attention, taking care it is conducted with the greatest regularity and economy;—to her the domestic servants of the Institution shall be immediately responsible for the performance of their respective duties:—and under the direction of the Ladies' Visiting Committee she shall have power to engage or discharge them.

II.—She shall take care of the household goods and furniture, according to the inventory, and be ready to give an account thereof when required; she shall superintend and assist in making and mending the linen articles belonging to the Institution, and see to the proper repairing of the children's clothing when brought in from the Laundry; and in these latter duties she shall be helped by the female assistant and the girls of the school.

III.—She shall visit the Dormitories and Offices frequently, and take care that the chambers are well ventilated; that the beds, clothes, linen and all other things and places in the house are kept clean, and that every child gets clean sheets when admitted, and that they be changed every fourteen days, or oftener if necessary;—whenever the weather will permit, she shall order a certain number of mattrasses, blankets and quilts, in rotation, to be exposed to the sun, and well aired, and the girls shall assist the servants in these and all other duties of the household.

IV.—She shall take care that the respective rooms are scoured with soap and warm water, as often as necessary, and that they be kept constantly clean by sweeping.

V.—She will have charge of the store room, and receive all provisions or stores purchased, and shall see that there is the quantity charged for, and that the quality is good, shall keep them under her own care, and deliver only such a quantity at a time as shall enable her to know that it is consumed. Books shall be kept with every tradesman employed, in which each article shall be entered at the time it is furnished; and nothing shall be sold or disposed of belonging to the Institution; that nothing is wasted or carried away; and she shall keep an account of her expenditure.

VI.—She shall be careful that the meals are provided as prescribed by the Diet Scale; shall superintend the preparing of them, and take care that they are served at regular stated hours, and see that none is wasted, and that no provisions are brought into the Institution, but such as the Committee prescribed.

VII.—She shall treat the children with good nature and civility, and she shall never suffer any degree of cruelty, insolence or neglect in the servants towards them to pass unnoticed.

VIII.—She shall keep a house journal in which shall be entered the daily proceedings of the house to be laid before the Committees at their meetings.

IX.—She will be required to lay before the Ladies' Committee a requisition of articles for the use of the Establishment, exhibiting for inspection all unserviceable articles, such requisition to be forwarded to the Secretary when approved of by the Ladies' Visiting Committee.

X.—She will keep a Book in which shall be entered all articles required for the use of the Institution.

XI.—The Matron and her Assistant shall attend Church alternately with the Protestant girls once each Sunday.

XII.—The Matron or her Assistant shall take the girls for a walk once a week.

XIII.—The Matron or Matron's Assistant shall not both be absent from the Institution at the same time.

XIV.—She will be required to muster for School, and inspect the children for cleanliness and neatness of dress, at 8.45 a.m., and 1.45 p.m., when she will distribute those allotted to their daily duties.

XV.—She will see that every child on admission is well bathed, &c., and receives clean clothing.

XVI.—She, or in her absence the Matron's Assistant, will receive all Visitors to the Institution, and conduct them over the Establishment.

XVII.—She will frequently inspect all Cooking Utensils, and see to their being in an efficient condition.

XVIII.—She will call in the Medical Officer in any cases of Sickness, and be responsible for the carrying out of his directions.

XIX.—In all matters not specified in these Rules, the Matron shall be directed by the Committee.

THE MATRON'S ASSISTANT.

I.—Shall be appointed by the Committee. She will assist in the Management immediately under the direction of the Matron.

II.—She will be present at the Bathing, Washing, and Combing of all the Children, and see to their Clothing being in good repair.

III.—She will be responsible as seamstress, for the making and repairing of Clothing, &c., by the girls; and will keep in order the Clothing Room—receiving the clean clothing from the laundry, and giving it out as required.

IV.—She will be required especially to supervise the Dormitories, that they and the Bedding are kept clean, well aired, and in good order.

V.—Will attend to the Children when going to Bed.

VI.—She will not absent herself from the Institution without permission having been previously obtained from the Matron.

VII.—She will see that all Clothing, Bedding, &c., is properly marked and numbered.

VIII.—She will superintend the scrubbing and cleaning of every portion of the Building—overlook the cleaning of the Dormitories, Bath Rooms, Committee and Visitors' Rooms, Passages and Staircase, Sitting and Bed Rooms, Hall and Door Steps, also School, and Dining Halls, and Offices.

IX.—She will lay the Table for Meals, and in the absence of either the Master or Matron, will preside during the same.

X.—She will attend specially to the Laundry department, and be careful that no soiled linen accumulate.

ASSISTANT TEACHERS.

I.—They shall be appointed by the Committee, and will be under the immediate control of the Master, from whom they will receive instructions relative to their duties in the School; also enforce good conduct during Play hours—and have the care of the Children out at doors at play.

II.—Will assist by all possible means in carrying out the Rules of the Institution and the instructions of the Superior Officers.

III.—Will report to the Master any Books or Materials required for the use of the Children under their care.

General Rules.

1.—The Master and Matron or in the absence of either, the officer next in charge will preside at all Meals, before and after which grace shall be sung and also repeated in the manual alphabet; and at all meals due decorum observed.

2.—Two or more of the girls shall be appointed each week, on Mondays, by the Matron to assist in housework, until not later than half-past ten o'clock in the forenoon, when they shall enter school;—except on Washing Day, (one day in the week,) when they may remain from school until two o'clock.

3.—Two or more of the boys shall be appointed each week by the Master to assist in house work, in the mornings until 10 o'clock a.m.

4.—The boys shall use the Bath on Sundays, Tuesdays, Thursdays, and Saturday Mornings, and the girls on Monday, Wednesday, and Friday mornings, before eight o'clock a.m., and Saturday Afternoons after three o'clock p.m.

5.—The Children are required to appear at all times clean and neat in their persons and dress.

6.—No Lights are to be left in their Dormitories excepting under special directions.

7.—The Girls shall assist in making and mending clothing, under the direction of the Matron and Matron's Assistant after School Hours.

8.—All Dormitory Windows are to be opened immediately upon the children arising, and to be kept open all day, except in bad weather.

9.—The Children are not permitted to be in the front portion of the grounds except when under the supervision of one of the Officers.

10.—The Boys must not go to the Girls' portion, or the Girls to the Boys' portion of the House or grounds, except in company of an Officer of the Institution.

11.—Smoking in any part of the premises, is strictly prohibited, and the possession of lucifer matches by the Children is not permitted.

12.—The Children shall have three meals a day—Breakfast, Dinner, and Supper, to consist of such articles and quantities as the Committee may from time to time direct, and the Scale of Diet, as prescribed, shall be strictly adhered to.

13.—The House Servants shall be under the control of the Matron, and shall not absent themselves without her permission.

14.—The Hours of attendance in School shall be from ten a.m. until four p.m. daily, with intermission as may be arranged by the Committee—Saturdays and Sundays excepted. Instruction shall be given from such books only as the Committee may decide, morality and obedience strictly enforced.

15.—The Servants of the Institution shall not be absent after nine o'clock p.m., nor any of the Officers after ten o'clock p.m., except by special permission of the Master.

16.—Evening Prayers shall be said by the Master for the whole establishment, every Sunday evening at 7 p.m., in Winter, at 8 p.m. in Summer.

17.—The Roman Catholic Children may attend their place of worship, in charge of an authorised person.

18.—No unnecessary Work shall be done on Sundays.

19.—All correspondence from the pupils to their friends, should pass through the Secretary's hands.

20.—Any infraction of any of the foregoing Rules, must be reported in writing by the Master to the Secretary.

By order,

Approved by the Committee,   ELLIS ROBINSON,
May, 1872.   *Hon. Secretary.*

No. _____

NEW SOUTH WALES
Institution for the Deaf & Dumb, & the Blind.

———o———

FORM OF RECOMMENDATION FOR ADMISSION.

1. State Christian Name and Surname, Age, and Religion of the Child recommended for admission, and Native Place..

2. State Christian Names and Surnames of the Father and Mother, also trade or calling, and present residence...................

3. State circumstances of the case ; also as to the amount that the Parents or Friends are able and willing to contribute towards the maintenance and education of the Child, and what security can be offered that such payments will be duly made.......................

Signature of two Subscribers to the Institution............ { 1
2

Signature of Clergyman or Magistrate of the District in which the Child resides...... { 3

Dated this _____ *day of* _____ 187

HISTORICAL STATEMENT of Candidate for Admission.

——o——

No._____

DEAF AND DUMB CHILDREN.

——o——

1. What is the Name of Candidate? ...|
2.   Age? ... ...
3.   Religion of Parents? ...
4.   Native place? ... ...
5.   Usual Residence? ... ...
6. Has   been afflicted from birth? ...
7. Is the affliction hereditary; i.e., by direct transmission from the Parents?
8. Is the affliction single or double? ...
9. Has the single or double affliction always been present? ... ...
10. Is the power to hear sounds entirely absent? ... ...
11. Is the power to utter articulate sounds entirely absent? ... ...
12. Has   had Measles, Whooping Cough, or Scarlet Fever? ... ...
13. Has   suffered from fright, grief, or other emotional causes? ... ...
14. Has   suffered from fits of any kind, fever, palsy, or injury to head or spine? ... ...
15. Are the parents in any degree related, if so, what is their consanguinity? ...
16. Does the Mother attribute the affliction to any circumstance occuring during her pregnancy? ... ...
17. Are any other members of the family or relatives of the Parents similarly afflicted? ... ...
18. What is the state of   intellect? ...
19. Is there any malformation of the interior of the mouth and throat? ...
20. State any peculiarities of stature, bodily configuration, &c. ... ...
21. Also whether the Parents are intemperate and profligate ... ...
22. Are any other children similarly afflicted known to the Parents as resident in their neighbourhood? ...
23. Are both Parents alive? ... ...
24. How many other Children are there in family besides the Candidate? ...

Date of Admission...........................   Date of Leaving...........................

HISTORICAL STATEMENT of Candidate for Admission.

———o———

BLIND CHILDREN. No._____

———o———

1. What is the Name of Candidate ? ...|_____

2.   Age and date of birthday?|

3.   Religion of Parents ? ...|

4.   Native place ? ... ...|

5.   Usual Residence ? ... ...|

6. Is the Sight entirely Gone ? ... ...|

7.   ,, Blindness Congenital ? ... ...|

8. If from accident or disease, describe the circumstances connected with the origin of the Blindness ? ... ...|

9. Has any Surgical Operation been performed for the relief of the Blindness?|

10. Is there any other defect of the senses?

11. Has   suffered from fits of any kind fever, palsy, or any injury to the head, face, or spine ? ... ...|

12. Has   had Measles, Whooping Cough, or Scarlet Fever ? ... ...|

13. Has   been Vaccinated ? ... ...|

14. Are the Parents in any degree Related, and if so, what is their Consanguinity ?|

15. Are any other members or relatives of the family similiary afflicted ? ... ...|

16. Does the Mother attribute the affliction to any circumstance occuring during her Pregnancy ? ... ...|

17. What is the state of   intellect ?...|

18. State any peculiarities of Stature, Bodily Configuration, &c. ... ...|

19. Also whether the Parents are intemperate or profligate ... ...|

20. Are any other children similarly afflicted, known to the Parents as resident in the neighbourhood ? ...|

21. How many other children are there in the family ? ... ...|

22. Are both Parents alive ? ... ...|

Date of Admission........................ Date of Leaving...........................

MEDICAL CERTIFICATE.

I certify that I have this day examined..and have found...........in good bodily health, and free from cutaneous and contagious disorders. I consider............a fit subject for admission to the Institution.   Date...........................18......

...Honorary Medical Officer.

FORM OF A BEQUEST

TO THE

New South Wales Institution for the Deaf and Dumb, and the Blind.

I give and bequeath unto A. B. (or unto my said Executors—or my said Trustees as the case may be) the sum of _____ upon trust to pay out of my Personal Estate to the Treasurer for the time being of "The New South Wales Institution for the Deaf and Dumb, and the Blind" such sum as a donation to the said Institution.

The following is the proper attestation to a Will :—

(Signatures and addresses.)

Signed by the above-named testator as and for his last Will in our presence who in his presence at his request and in the presence of each other have sub-scribed our names as witnesses.

TABULAR STATEMENT OF NAMES &c., of CHILDREN who have been Pupils of the Institution

from the Foundation 1860, until September, 1874.

DEAF AND DUMB CHILDREN.

No.	Name.	Age on Admission.	Religion.	Where Received from.	Date of Admission	Date of Leaving	Other Children in family. *Most of these Children were received into the Institution on opening. From the length of time elapsed it is difficult to obtain information about them.*	Remarks.
1	Lorsey, Patrick	...	Roman Catholic	Sydney, N.S.W.	...	...		Apprentice to a Shoemaker.
2	Thorp, Joseph	...	Ditto	Ditto	...	...		
3	Hagen, Felix	14	Ditto	Ditto	1860	...		Died.
4	Patterson, Henry	...	Protestant	Shoallhaven	...	...		Taken to Benevolent Asylum.—Idiotic.
5	Lentz, Anne	...	Ditto	Sydney	...	...		Only a short time a pupil.
6	Hurst, Susan	14	Ditto	Ditto	1860	1862		Returned to friends.
7	Poulton, William	...	Ditto	Ditto	...	...		
8	Carmichael, Edward	11	Roman Catholic	Ditto	1860	...		
9	Bridgement, Annie	4	Protestant	Ditto	1860	Feb. 1864		Went to Scotland.
10	Plowright, Selina	12	Ditto	Ditto	1860	Sept. 1863		Since died.
11	Pearson, Elizabeth	17	Ditto	Ditto	1860	June 1864		
12	Morrow, William	9	Ditto	Camperdown	Jan. 1860	Jan. 1864		Gone to a trade—Coach Painter.
13	Logan, Thomas	10	Ditto	Sydney	May 1863	1866		
14	Murray, Richard	5	Roman Catholic	Ditto	Aug. 1863	1864		
15	Mailley, Harriet	14	Protestant	Ditto	Jan. 1862	Jan. 1864		
16	Keene, Lizzie	12	Roman Catholic	Ditto	1860	1867		Went to Brisbane.
17	Lynch, Deborah	8	Protestant	Ditto	1860	1864		Returned to her friends.
18	Gleadhill, Mary Jane	14	Ditto	Picton	1863	April 1864		Living with her friends.
19	Hill, Emma	9	Ditto	Sydney	1860	1866		In service now.
20	Mailley, Richard	13	Ditto	Ditto	Jun. 1865	Jan. 1865		
21	Smith, Thomas	14	Ditto	Hinton, Hunter River	1860	1864		Returned to his friends.
22	McLaughlin, Richard	15	Ditto	Warialda, N.S.W.	Feb. 1862	May 1864		

No.	Name	Age	Religion	Place	Admitted		Discharged		No.	Remarks
23	McLaughlin, Thomas	12	Protestant	Warialda, N.S.W.	Feb.	1862	May	1864	...	Returned to his friends.
24	Lewis, William	13	Ditto	Pyrmont, Sydney	Oct.	1862	Dec.	1865	...	Absconded.
25	Hart, Elizabeth	16	Ditto	New Zealand	Feb.	1862	Mar.	1866	...	Returned to New Zealand.
26	Bates, Kate	11	Roman Catholic	Sofala, N.S.W.	Dec.	1861	Dec.	1865	...	Went to service.
27	Kelly, Eleanor	11	Ditto	Appin	April	1861	June	1869	9	Returned to her friends.
28	Wright, Christiana J.	11	Ditto	Sydney	Feb.	1862	Sep.	1865	...	Ditto ditto.
29	Thompson, Jane	7	Unitarian	Parramatta	„	1862	Oct.	1873	4	Ditto ditto.
30	Egglestone, William	5	Protestant	Shellharbour	Aug.	1862	...	...	4	Now in the Institution.
31	Richardson, William	11	Ditto	Richmond	Jan.	1862	June	1866	4	Went to a trade—Saddler.
32	Waterson, Rebecca	10	Ditto	Concord	Nov.	1864	Mar.	1865	1	Was Idiotic & taken to an Asylum for insane.
33	Thompson, Mary Ann	10	Ditto	Fitzroy Iron Mines	Feb.	1865	Feb.	1872	4	Sent to Newcastle Institution for Imbeciles.
34	Golding, Mary Jane	10	Ditto	Irish Town, N.S.W.	May.	1865	...	...	8	Now in the Institution.
35	Farmer, William	11	Ditto	Newcastle, ditto	Nov.	1865	...	...	8	Gone to work at a Coal Mine.
36	McKenzie, Catherine	13	Ditto	Wentworth, ditto	July	1865	...	...	6	Returned to friends.
37	Morrison, William	16	Ditto	Nerigunda, ditto	July	1865	Nov.	1868	...	„ „
38	Milner, Alfred Herbert	13	Ditto	Broadwater, Namoi R.	Dec.	1865	Jan.	1870	...	„ „
39	Sullivan, Catherine	6	Roman Catholic	Bathurst, N.S.W.	Jan.	1866	...	...	...	„ „
40	Cameron, Christina	9	Protestant	Goulburn, ditto	Feb.	1866	...	...	4	Now in the Institution—Teacher.
41	Stewart, Mary Anne	13	Ditto	Lachlan, ditto	Feb.	1866	May	1869	6	Returned to her friends.
42	Eggleston, Mary Anne	5	Ditto	Shellharbour, ditto	May	1866	...	...	4	Now in the Institution.
43	Wearne, Anne Susan	5	Ditto	Newcastle, ditto	Aug.	1866	...	...	1	„ „
44	Singer, Louisa Sophia	15	Ditto	Hobart Town, Tasmania	Sept.	1866	Sept.	1871	9	Returned to her friends.
45	Love, Thomas	12	Ditto	Rockhampton, Queensld.	Nov.	1866	Nov.	1871	5	Gone to a trade—Shoemaker.
46	Smart, Albert	8	Ditto	Sydney	July	1867	...	...	3	Ditto ditto—Cabinetmaker.
47	Ryder, Henrietta	18	Ditto	Windsor, N.S.W.	Aug.	1867	...	...	5	Left the Institution.
48	Pollock, Alexander	10	Ditto	King's Plains, Queensld.	Jan.	1868	...	...	5	Now in the Institution.
49	Saber, Barnard	12	Hebrew	Sydney	Sept.	1868	...	...	8	Gone to a Trade—Jeweller.
50	Walsh, Thomas	13	Roman Catholic	Ditto	Nov.	1868	...	...	3	Taken away by his friends.
51	Murphy, John	11	Ditto	Ipswich, Queensland	April	1869	...	...	3	Returned to Brisbane.
52	Jamison, Archibald	6	Protestant	Ditto, ditto	Jan.	1869	...	...	4	Now in the Institution.
53	Hurst, Edwin	6	Ditto	Sydney	Feb.	1869	...	...	4	„ „
54	Jordon, Daniel William	6	Protestant	Queanbeyan	April	1869	...	...	4	„ „
55	Jordon, Charles	4	Ditto	Ditto	„	1869	...	...	4	„ „
56	Byrnes, William	8	Roman Catholic	New England, N.S.W.	„	1869	...	...	4	Left the Institution.

TABULAR STATEMENT OF NAMES, &c.—Continued.

DEAF AND DUMB CHILDREN.—Continued.

No.	Name.	Age on Admission.	Religion.	Where Received from.	Date of Admission.	Date of Leaving.	Other Children in family.	Remarks.
57	Smuils, Susan	9	Protestant	Manning River	May 1869	...	5	Now in the Institution.
58	Coles, Mary Isabel	7	Ditto	Sydney	July 1869	...	1	"
59	Smithers, Thomas	7	Ditto	Araluen	Nov. 1866	Dec. 1866	...	Idiotic & removed to Asylum for Insane.
60	Selby, John	9	Ditto	Auckland, New Zealand	May 1869	...	7	Now in the Institution.
61	Farr, Arthur Thomas	5	Ditto	Redfern, N.S.W.	May 1869	...	4	"
62	Sparke, Maria Goldfinch	10	Ditto	West Maitland, N.S.W.	Oct. 1869	...	10	"
63	Boulton, Adelaide Rosine	11	Ditto	McLeay River, N.S.W.	Jun. 1870	May 1871	3	Returned to her friends to Victoria.
64	Jessip, Emmeline	9	Ditto	Ryde, Parramatta River	" 1870	...	6	"
65	Chapman, Bridget	5	Ditto	Sydney	June 1870	...	2	Now in the Institution.
66	Churchill, Emma Deborah	10	Ditto	Port McQuarie	Aug. 1870	...	7	"
67	Howe, Frederick	10	Ditto	Newtown, N.S.W.	Sep. 1870	...	1	"
68	Carpenter, John Thomas	7	Ditto	Ryde, Parramatta River	Oct. 1870	Nov. 1870	2	Idiotic and returned to his friends.
69	McDonald, Augustus John	8	Ditto	Concord, ditto	Jan. 1871	...	1	Now in the Institution.
70	Bridgement, Anna Elizab.	12	Ditto	Sydney, N.S.W.	Feb. 1871	July 1874	4	Returned to her friends.
71	Briteheno, Halston Elizab.	6	Ditto	Waterloo, N.S.W.	Mar. 1871	...	1	Now in the Institution.
72	Hurst, Herbert	7	Ditto	Wollongong	July 1871	...	4	"
73	Durham, John Edwin	5	Ditto	Singleton, N.S.W.	Jan. 1872	...	4	"
74	D'Arcy, William	7	Roman Catholic	Sydney	Feb. 1872	...	2	"
75	Arrell, Henry	11	Protestant	Brisbane, Queensland	Mar. 1872	...	6	"
76	Smith, Henry Caulfield	9	Ditto	Newtown	Mar. 1872	...	6	"
77	Jordan, Eliza Jane	6	Ditto	Queanbeyan	April 1872	Dec. 1873	5	Idiotic—taken to Newcastle Asylum.
78	McLaughlen, Frank	12	Ditto	Goorah, N.S.W.	" 1872	...	7	Now in the Institution.
79	Cameron, Lachlan	9	Ditto	Goulburn	May 1872	...	6	"
80	Rodgers, Ellen	9	Roman Catholic	Coolac, N.S.W.	Sept. 1872	...	6	"
81	Goldsworthy, James	8	Protestant	Adelaide, S.A.	" 1872	...	0	"
82	Harriss, Laura Evn	9	Ditto	Wollombi, N.S.W.	" 1872	...	4	"
83	White, Ida	5	Ditto	Merriwa, ditto	" 1872	...	1	"

No.	Name	Age	Religion	Place		Date		No.	Now in the Institution.
84	Weirman, Adolph	9	Protestant	Ipswich, Queensland		Sept.	1872	1	Now in the Institution.
85	Ruwald, Elizabeth Mary	10	Roman Catholic	Newcastle, N.S.W.		Feb.	1873	5	,,
86	Jones, Martha	8	Protestant	Clarence Town, ditto		,,	1873	4	,,
87	Jones, Annie	6	Ditto	Ditto ditto, ditto		,,	1873	6	,,
88	Smith, Margaret	18	Ditto	South Creek, ditto		,,	1873	1	,,
89	King, Margaret	9	Roman Catholic	Queensland		Aug.	1873	9	,,
90	Ryan, Mary Anne	13	Ditto	Hobart Town, Tasmania		Aug.	1873	2	,,
91	Ransley, Clara	12	Protestant	,,		June	1874	10	,,
92	Fitzpatrick, James	6	Roman Catholic	Moruya, N.S.W.	,,	Aug.	1871	3	,,
93	Wilbow, George	11	Protestant	Moonby,	,,	,,	1874	3	,,

BLIND CHILDREN.

No.	Name	Age	Religion	Place	Date				No.	Remarks
1	Adams, Edmund	13	Protestant	Newtown	Mar.	1869	Dec.	1870	11	Returned to his friends.
2	Worsley, Sarah Ann	10	Ditto	Camperdown	,,	1869	Mar.	1874	3	her ,,
3	Saunders, John W.	8	Ditto	Ieely Copper Mines	,,	1869			1	Now in the Institution.
4	Whannell, James A.	8	Ditto	Sydney, N.S.W.	Aug.	1869	Jan.	1870	3	Left the Colony.
5	Driscoll, John B.	13	Ditto	Rockhampton	Sept.	1869	,,	1874	3	Gone to a Trade.
6	McQuade, Susan Teresa	5	Roman Catholic	Sydney	Nov.	1869			2	Now in the Institution.
7	Ellis, John Frank	10	Protestant	Singleton, N.S.W.	Jan.	1870			3	,,
8	Allison, George Robert	8	Ditto	Brisbane, Queensland	May	1870			3	,,
9	Todd, Mary Jane	5	Ditto	Rockhampton	Jun.	1871			0	,,
10	Kluga, Mary Anne	6	Roman Catholic	Grenfel, N.S.W.,	June	1871			2	,,
11	Hicks, Mary Ann	6	Protestant	Bowen, Queensland	Sept.	1872			1	,,
12	Smith, Anne	10	Ditto	Braidwood	,,	1872			4	,,
13	Grube, John	9	Ditto	Sydney	,,	July	1873	Jan 1874	4	Returned to her friends.
14	Everingham, Henrietta	12	Ditto	Windsor, N.S.W.	,,	1873			7	Now in the Institution.
15	Mercer, Thomas	9	Ditto	Tasmania.	,,	1874			0	,,

Note.—A reference to the tables will show that 108 Children, 93 Deaf and Dumb, and 15 Blind, (55 Male and 54 Female) have been received into the Institution. Of these 56 have left to return to their friends and homes. 6 were found to be Idiotic, and beyond the influence of education, and were removed to Asylums for Insane. 53 now remain in the Institution. In ten of the families there are two or more deaf and dumb. 91 of the children are from New South Wales, 12 from Queensland, 2 from New Zealand, 3 from Tasmania, and 1 from Adelaide, South Australia.

THE DUMB CHILD.

She is my only girl.
I asked for her as some most precious thing,
For all unfinished was love's jewell'd ring
    Till set with this soft Pearl.   [see,
The shade that time brought forth I could not
So pure, so perfect, seemed the gift to me.

Oh! many a soft old tune
I used to sing unto that deaden'd ear,
And suffered not the slightest footstep near,
    Lest she might wake too soon :   [lay.
And hush'd her brother's laughter while she
Ah! needless care, I might have let them play.

'Twas long ere I believed
That this one daughter might not speak to me,
Waited and watched, GOD knows how patiently
    How willingly deceived.
Vain love was long the untiring nurse of faith,
And tended hope, until it starved to death.

Oh! if she could but hear   [teach,
For one short hour that I her tongue might
To call me Mother in the broken speech,
    That thrills the Mother's ear.
Alas, those sealed lips never may be stirred,
To the deep music of that lovely word.

My heart it sorely tries,
To see her kneel with such a reverend air,
Beside her brothers at their evening prayer—
    Or lift those earnest eyes   [knew,
To watch our lips, as though our words she
Then move her own, as she were speaking too.

I've watched her looking up
To the bright wonder of an evening sky,
With such a depth of meaning in her eye,
    That I could almost hope   [cords,
The struggling soul would burst its binding
And the long pent up thought flow forth in
        [words.

The song of bird and bee,
The chorus of the breezes, streams, and groves,
All the great music to which nature moves,
    Are wasted melody.
To her—the world of sound a timeless void,
While even silence hath its charm destroyed.

Her face is very fair,
Her blue eye beautiful,—of finest mould
Her soft white brow on which in waves of gold,
    Ripples her shining hair :
Alas! this lovely temple closed must be,
For He who made it keeps the master key.

Wills He the mind within,   [free.
Should from earth's clamour—Babel be kept
E'en that His " Still small voice " and step
    Heard at its inner shrine,   [might be
Through that deep hush of soul with clearer
        [thrill.
Thou—should I grieve ? Oh ! murmuring heart
        [be still.

She seems to have a sense
Of quiet gladness in her noiseless play,
She has a pleasant smile a gentle way,
    Whose voiceless eloquence
Touches all hearts, though I had once the fear,
That even her father would not care for her.

Thank God! it is not so :
And when his sons are playing merrily,
She comes and leans her head upon his knee ;
    Oh ! at such times I know,
By the full eye, and tone subdued and mild,
How his heart yearns over his silent child.

Not of all gifts bereft,
E'en now how could I say she did not speak.
What real language lights her eye and cheek,
    In thanks to Him who left
Unto her soul yet open avenues,
For joy to enter and for love to use.

And GOD in love doth give
To her defect a beauty of its own,
And we a deeper tenderness have shown,
    Through that for which we grieved,
Yet shall the seal be melted from the ear,
Yea, and my voice shall fill it,—but not here.

When that new sense is given,
What rapture will its first experience be,
That never woke to meaner melody,
    Than the rich songs of Heaven :
To hear the full tuned anthem swelling round,
While angels teach the extacies of sound.
               ANONYMOUS.

MANUAL ALPHABET.

Double Hand.

As used at the Institution.